Welsh Boxing Annual 2019-2020

Dewi Powell

Copyright © 2020 Dewi Powell

All rights reserved. The right of Dewi Powell to be identified as the author of this work has been asserted in accordance with the Copyright Design and Patents Act 1988.

No part of this book may be reproduced in any form or by any means, electronic or mechanical, including photocopying, recording, or by any information storage and retrieval system without permission in writing from the author.

ISBN: 9798694164849

ACKNOWLEDGEMENTS

For better or worse, boxing isn't like other sports. There are few barriers to access and, unlike football or rugby, the press officers that writers occasionally encounter are often helpful enablers. When the bravado is bypassed, boxers can be the most incredibly authentic subjects and they're often honest to a fault.

Boxing's openness, on and off the record, is a writer's bliss. It's demonstrated by the fact that every interview in this book was accepted at the first request and without any conditions. That deserves credit, especially in the climate of carefully managed spokespeople in the public eye. I'm thankful to every interviewee who has afforded their time to this project.

This book benefits from the generosity of four photographers. They are Huw Fairclough, Liam Hartery, Spencer Love and Sacha Wiener. All of them offered help without any hesitation and I'm very grateful for it. The people and moments on the following pages are brought to life by the colour the quartet have contributed.

My final, and foremost, thanks go to my family. Chlöe, my fiancé, is a long-suffering boxing widow. Her role as my sense checker and sounding board has been an invaluable source of support. I also owe a debt to my parents, Paul and Sonia, that I'll never be able to repay.

- Dewi Powell

ABOUT THE AUTHOR

Dewi Powell was born in Caerphilly, South Wales and has written about boxing for a decade. In that time, he has contributed to local newspapers and trade press, including the South Wales Argus and Boxing News, and set up BoxingWales.com in 2012.

After graduating in journalism from the University of Central Lancashire, Dewi moved to Cardiff and has since worked in public sector communications. He spends most of his spare time walking his dog, Hallie.

He can be found on social media @DewiPowell and will gladly accept your feedback.

REVIEWS

Andy Clarke, Sky Sports commentator

"Boxing is a sport of record. It's essential that good records are kept and for that you need chroniclers you can trust. And Dewi Powell is exactly that person. He doesn't just tell you who won and by what method but also what happened, in what circumstances and what the result meant in a wider context. Having an annual like this is great for fighters and fans alike. I really hope it's the first of many."

Tris Dixon, journalist and host of Boxing Life Stories podcast

"The biggest mistake you can make about the Welsh Boxing Annual 2019-2020 is that it's merely a record book. It's more than that, it's the definitive journey through the sport through 12 months covering all of boxing's bases. Stories of 'fixed fights', world title contests, Olympic qualification, the impact of coronavirus, performance enhancing drugs, upsets, controversies and good, hard contests, it's all in there in graphic detail with access to the country's biggest names and a ringside seat to their biggest fights. Every chapter is different but equally illuminating. Don't be mistaken in thinking that this book is only for aficionados of Welsh boxing. That does it a disservice. It's a well-written diary of a year covering the dramatic highs and lows the sport always offers."

Michael Pearlman, BBC Sport Wales journalist

"Dewi Powell's passion, knowledge and understanding of Welsh boxing is unsurpassed and permeates every page of this bible for Welsh fight fans. There is no such thing as a dull year in Welsh boxing but the Welsh Boxing Annual 2019-2020 captures a period that was unlike any other. From world title fights to Olympic amateur aspirations dashed, Dewi documents a tumultuous time in a love letter to a nation with boxing in its blood."

Anson Wainwright, The Ring Magazine journalist

"An all-encompassing and nostalgic look back at the Welsh boxing scene. It evokes some wonderful memories from the grassroots levels and small hall venues all the way up to the world scene. Journeymen, local ticket sellers, fledgling prospects, domestic and world-rated contenders, all the way up to past and hopefully future Welsh world champions, you'll find them all here. Wales isn't and never has lacked for talented prize-fighters. A must read for all Welsh boxing fans."

ACRONYMS

ABC	Amateur Boxing Club
AIBA	International Boxing Association
BBBoC	British Boxing Board of Control
COVID-19	Coronavirus disease (SARS-CoV-2)
DCMS	Department for Digital, Culture, Media and Sport
EBU	European Boxing Union
IBF	International Boxing Federation
IOC	International Olympic Committee
MMA	Mixed Martial Arts
PEDs	Performance enhancing drugs
PPE	Personal protective equipment
VADA	Voluntary Anti-Doping Association
WADA	World Anti-Doping Agency
WBA	World Boxing Association
WBC	World Boxing Council
WBO	World Boxing Organisation
WEBA	Welsh Ex-Boxer's Association
WHO	World Health Organisation
UFC	Ultimate Fighting Championship
UKAD	United Kingdom Anti-Doping

CONTENTS

1	Introduction	Pg 1
2	Dragone undone by suspect scoring as Touze crowned Welsh champion	Pg 3
3	Jones downed but rises to overcome Anthony and win Welsh title	Pg 6
4	Dixon given birthday bruises as he shreds ring rust	Pg 9
5	Six straightforward wins on Sanigar Events undercard	Pg 11
6	Dropped Davies bounces back to beat Chelli	Pg 13
7	Priority Boxing plant a flag in the capital	Pg 15
8	Thunder Thorley returns to restart career	Pg 18
9	Selby shines… and then survives serious scare	Pg 20
10	Last minute disruption doesn't ruffle Robinson	Pg 22
11	World Championship medal escapes Eccles' reach in Russia	Pg 24
12	Harris breaks down Barnes in Belfast with world level in his sights	Pg 26
13	Price claims world crown to create history	Pg 29
14	Dixon does himself proud on Italian away day	Pg 31
15	Selby keeps world title hopes alive in clash of former world champions	Pg 34
16	Ex-Selby opponent is free to fight after positive drug test	Pg 38
17	Edwards and Woodruff with third round thrashings at York Hall	Pg 40

18	Williams goes from Clydach to the ~~Congo~~ Copper Box	Pg 43
19	Gething goes out of Golden Contract tournament	Pg 46
20	Evans eventually succumbs to Tennyson in fight of the year contender	Pg 59
21	Jenkins' title defence cut short by head clashes	Pg 52
22	Classy Cordina makes mini-statement in Monte Carlo	Pg 56
23	Gwynne's quick KO sets up another shot at the British title	Pg 59
24	Sanigar Events showcase small hall talent in Gwent	Pg 62
25	Olympian Evans rekindles his hunger and unbeaten Thomas ticks on	Pg 64
26	Calzaghe's career celebrated with lifetime achievement award	Pg 68
27	Lockett's stable increases unbeaten streak to meet milestone	Pg 70
28	Yaxley and Warburton intend to put North Wales on the boxing map	Pg 74
29	Fox hunter Williams sets up world title shot	Pg 76
30	Harris' chance for dream world title confirmed	Pg 81
31	Welsh Area Council honour award winners	Pg 85
32	Qualifying opportunities confirmed for trio of Olympic hopefuls	Pg 88
33	Fixed fight? Betting controversy overshadows Darch defeat	Pg 92
34	Edwards steps up in style to see-off Phillips	Pg 95
35	Drained Davies suffers defeat to inspired Sadiq	Pg 98

36	Harris earns hero status in world title challenge	Pg 102
37	WHO declare global pandemic but boxing beats on	Pg 107
38	The only show in town	Pg 109
39	North Wales trio stay busy and build towards homecoming	Pg 112
40	Out, injured, postponed: Olympic qualification avoids Welsh trio	Pg 115
41	COVID-19 lockdown cancels the calendar	Pg 118
42	Mohammed Hashim Jeéracks mourned after tragic death	Pg 122
43	Omar opts for new path as professional prizefighter	Pg 123
44	Selby's world title eliminator succumbs to COVID-19, again	Pg 126
45	Project restart: Business as unusual	Pg 130
46	Turf war! Tennyson takes out Gwynne in garden showdown	Pg 134
47	Thorley's unbeaten bubble burst in Billam-Smith shootout	Pg 139
48	Thomas tamed in battle of unbeaten prospects	Pg 141
49	Underdog Hughes upsets 'King Kong' Carroll	Pg 144
50	Weetch on the wrong end of early knockout	Pg 148
51	Woodruff comes close against clever Cully	Pg 150
52	Final thoughts	Pg 153

INTRODUCTION

Welcome to the inaugural Welsh Boxing Annual and thank you for supporting this new project.

The traditional boxing 'season' used to run from the start of September to the end of July. The old schedule would afford August to those in the sport who needed some time to rest and recover from the rat race, before it restarted and ran again. Nowadays, not even one month is spared and the boxing beat thumps continuously all year long. The constant 365-day cycle is largely due to ever-increasing demand dictated by broadcasters, venue availability and, more importantly, the energy from within the sport itself.

For the purpose of an annual review, this book honours the timescale of the traditional season and documents the events from September 2019 to September 2020. The ups and down of Wales' professional boxers and elite amateurs are covered as they unfold, providing a chronological timeline from the frontline. All of the important stories from across the country and beyond are told through a series of features, interviews and reports from ringside. A spotlight is shone on the main people at the centre of these stories.

As this book begins, several Welsh boxers are about to compete internationally. Wales entered the 2019-2020 season without a world champion and hopes were held that the 13th world champion would emerge from a population of just over three million people. The optimism came from the belts already held on Welsh soil; three Commonwealth and four British titles in total. There was justified reason to believe the current crop of Welsh boxers had the ability to compete above their collective weight, as their forebearers have done through history. Appetites for Welsh titles were whetted more than usual on the home front, too. Despite the main promoters in the United Kingdom [UK] showing little interest in Wales, two English-based promotional entities kept Welsh boxers busy with regular shows hosted in small halls.

Some of the themes in this book are controversial; performance enhancing drugs [PEDs], questionable officiating and claims of fixed fights all make an appearance. A large section is also dominated by the disruption and death caused by coronavirus disease [COVID-19/SARS-CoV-2]. However, there is plenty of positivity and perhaps the best example of that is the new era emerging in the amateur ranks. Two women, who rose to the top of amateur boxing, had their sights set on earning Olympic glory. Their ambition could inspire generations of female fighters on boxing's modernising landscape, where both sexes are starting to be given more equal and overdue recognition.

Although written in the third person, many of the events in this book were witnessed in the first person. My name is Dewi Powell and I've written about Welsh boxers since 2010. In the decade since, I've contributed to local newspapers and trade magazines, and set up the BoxingWales.com website. The reason I've written this book, its purpose, is to allow readers to vividly relive the memories of Welsh boxing. Nothing like this has, to my knowledge, been done in Welsh boxing before and I've aimed to chronicle everything worth knowing in the 2019-2020 season.

Our country's fighting history deserves to be recognised in its future, whether this is read on the day its published or in the years to come. The following pages are written in tribute to today's punchers, who fly the flag at home and abroad, ensuring our niche sport continues to survive and thrive.

DRAGONE UNDONE BY SUSPECT SCORING AS TOUZE CROWNED WELSH CHAMPION
Friday 13 September 2019

Carmarthen's Angelo Dragone (5-1) left the ring feeling wronged after losing a disputed decision to Swansea's Kristian Touze (9-0-2), who became Welsh super-featherweight champion at the end of 10 enthralling rounds.

The West Walian derby grew into a big attraction amongst locals in the area, enticing terrestrial channel S4C to broadcast the Sanigar Events show live from the LC2 venue in Swansea. 30 minutes of ferocious fighting lived up to the occasion and the only disappointment came when Master of Ceremonies Ricky Wright read the controversial verdict. Referee Reece Carter somehow submitted a 97-94 scorecard to award the vacant crown to Touze.

"I give my all. I wear my heart on my sleeve," said Dragone, who passes those principles on as coach to a community of gym-goers. "It felt like I done enough and obviously my cornermen were confident. I was really confident of winning and when I heard the scorecard go against me, it was a very bitter pill to swallow.

"I'm a down to earth guy. I've got a kids academy and stuff like that. I build the respect and discipline for the sport into them. There's no point acting like a sore loser. Dust yourself down and go again. It's not about throwing my toys out of the pram like some people would."

The official announcement was greeted by some cheers and a louder chorus of disapproving jeers. Many fans objected to a verdict that credited just three rounds to a dominant Dragone. Boxing was never shy of controversy and this was certainly one of the most memorable incidents in Welsh boxing for a number of years, albeit for the wrong reasons.

Dragone was in hot pursuit from the opening bell and he managed to close the distance quickly, firing away short hooks to the body. Southpaw Touze, leading with his right hand and holding his left further back, tried to pot shot in response. When Dragone got past the jabs, Touze then attempted to tie him up and skip away for longer-range exchanges. The action didn't slow in the second round and a straight right hand bloodied Touze's nose. It wasn't the last time claret would be shed. Before the round was out, an accidental head clash left him bleeding from a cut above his eyebrow. Dragone looked too strong and even when his blatant aggression resulted in him taking the occasional single shot, Touze couldn't slow Dragone's relentless attacks.

Touze had his first stint of success in the fourth round, managing to score with straight punches and then smother Dragone at close quarters. However, it was short lived and Dragone re-imposed himself soon after. The only interruptions came when Touze shrewdly spoilt the action. Now it was Dragone's turn to bleed and a wound opened up below his left eye in the middle rounds, soon followed by a symmetrical cut under his right eye. Touze was used to handing out cuts on a day-to-day basis but these were accidental, caused when the barber unintentionally clashed heads.

Dragone said: "[It was the] first time I'd been cut. They were both identical, from head clashes. It didn't phase me at all, to be honest.

"I didn't know what was going on. I went back to the corner and Richie [Garner – trainer and manager] put a bit of adrenaline in my eye and it stung. I was like, 'Fuck! What was that?' I thought he was going to put Vaseline on it.

"If they [the cuts] were over my eyes, the ref could've called it [off] but because they were under my eyes, it didn't affect them at all. They were quite deep."

The sight of Dragone's blood inspired Touze into action, helping him to bank the seventh round with well-timed counters. The sheer effort and admirable concentration helped Touze to stop the rot and give his corner, headed by David John, hope of turning the tide. Then the eighth session was an undoubted contender for round of the year. Both took turns to unload on each other, nearing the point of exhaustion. The only difference between them was Dragone's strength, which appeared to give him front foot leverage.

A boisterous atmosphere accompanied the boxers in the ninth and 10th rounds. The spontaneity spurred Dragone and Touze to empty their respective tanks in the closing stages. Sound bounced around the hall and the duo earned enormous credit from a very vocal crowd. Emotions were high during the derby but the crowd's conduct remained relatively peaceful afterwards.

Keen to acknowledge the unforgettable support, Dragone said: "I felt the crowd the whole fight, it was a big impact. There was a huge crowd there and when they said the decision in the room… the room emptied. I've never heard boos like that before at a small hall show. Mental, wasn't it?

"It was a toe to toe fight all the way through. It was 10 rounds of non-stop action. The crowd was awesome from round one to round 10. I remember getting off my stool for the 10th round and the racket was unbelievable."

Naturally, Dragone disagreed with the decision. He took it gracefully and welcomed his two children to the ring. They were raised to Dragone's shoulders to free his arms and so he could salute an army of fans. The former milkman had exceeded the expectations set when he turned professional after a modest amateur career.

Touze was exhausted and ecstatic, all at the same time. The former serviceman was draped in a Welsh title as champion of his country. Regardless of the opinions of the referee's tally, Touze had given everything and won a ton of respect for his persistence. He was unlikely to grant a rematch, though this was now his night for celebration.

"From the start, I tried to pick him off, keep moving. I knew he was going to be aggressive and come forward all the time," analysed Touze as he sat on the edge of the ring apron and spoke to the S4C commentary team. "It was an amazing fight. He's still a champ himself.

"I've seen a couple of his fights, he's seen a couple of mine. I knew he wasn't going to change his style, I knew he was working with boys to cut me off, pressure me. He wanted to stop me in the later rounds, like he said, but I knew I had the fitness in the bag. Thank God for the outcome."

The fight raised one important, broader issue: whether or not a referee should also be the sole scoring judge of a 10 round fight. Some small hall promoters argue against the costs of having three judges when their financial margins are already so narrow. Others argue that given the 'snakes and ladders' nature of the business of boxing, the cost of a bad decision to a boxer's career far outweighs the cost of three judges. Dragone, who wanted to go on and defend the Welsh title against Lance Cooksey before Christmas, was an example of that. The latter, and larger, group of people wish to share the burden of scoring to relieve pressure on the referee and ensure that the best boxer wins. It wasn't to say bad decisions cease to exist when three judges are used, though logic suggested the likelihood would be lessened.

The underlying issue was the status of Welsh titles, officially classed as 'Area' titles by the British Boxing Board of Control [BBBoC]. The same issue affected Scottish and Northern Irish titles, akin to the Southern Area or Central Areas of England. BBBoC rules required just one referee to score area title fights, regardless of the strain put on referees who also have to keep the action under control. In contrast, English titles were classed as 'National' titles and have benefitted from three judges since Tyson Fury's controversial decision win against John McDermott in 2009. The contradiction showed no sign of changing no matter how difficult it was to justify.

It wasn't the last time this debate would rumble on… in fact, it took about an hour to return.

Photo: Sacha Wiener

JONES DOWNED BUT RISES TO OVERCOME ANTHONY AND WIN WELSH TITLE
Friday 13 September 2019

Aberdare's Morgan Jones (13-2, 5KO) climbed off the canvas to capture the vacant Welsh super-middleweight title with a hard-fought 97-95 decision win over Ammanford's Jake Anthony (6-1).

The pair went back-and-forth over 10 rounds and there was little to separate them in the second Welsh title fight of Sanigar Events' packed out show in Swansea, following Kristian Touze and Angelo Dragone's super-featherweight scorcher.

It was a career-saving win for Jones. The 28-year-old was recovering from repeat defeats in his last two outings, having been stopped and dropped over the course of 14 combined rounds. Overcoming the test presented by unbeaten Anthony boosted Jones' confidence and resurrected his hopes of making a major mark in boxing.

"I needed them [losses] in order to make it through the fight with Jake," he candidly confessed. "It was definitely the most important fight of my career.

"Winning the fight has kept my hopes of really progressing and making a name for myself in the sport, which is what I want to do still.

"Losing the fight against Jake would've put me in the journeyman category. I would've willingly taken that role if I'd lost the fight. I'd have still boxed but it's not boxing with the same heart."

They sized each other up in a tentative opener, then Jones and Anthony took it in turns to test the waters. Neither overcommitted as Jones jabbed and Anthony looked for the body by sending inquisitive hooks around the sides.

Anthony made a major breakthrough at the end of the second round. After a few minutes of prodding and poking, he detonated a huge right hand when Jones leaned back on to the ropes. Jones was stunned and fell to his knees. He took his time and looked to the corner, before getting up and using all of his experience to survive a follow up attack.

"I showed my resilience," Jones declared. "It was a really good shot. My mind was firmly on victory and that's what pulled me through that moment. It was never a doubt in my mind that I'd lose the fight.

"Going into the fight, I don't know if scared was the right word but lets just say I was very nervous of Jake's power because he's very strong. Even with that in my head, I couldn't see me losing the fight. It's just one of them intangible things in boxing."

The hunt was back on in the third round. Anthony menacingly launched overhands and Jones tried to fend him off with snappy straight shots. The defence was breached again in the third round, though Jones endured it with more stability. Early in the fourth round, Jones caught the eye with snappy uppercuts and he began to measure his punches with more precision. It left him open to replies but the pair were now exchanging on more even terms. The development was much to the delight of Jones' cornerman Paul Paveltish, affectionately known as Pebbles.

The fifth round saw more success for Jones until a cut opened on the edge of his left eye. Referee Martin Williams ruled that it was caused by an accidental clash of heads. Anthony, spurred on by coach Richie Garner, could literally smell blood and was energised for the remainder of the session. The pace slightly slowed in the following round and Chris Sanigar, working on cuts in Jones' corner, was managing to stem the bloody cut. Both appeared more speculative and seemed to welcome the opportunity to catch a breath.

Soon after in the seventh round, Anthony's power appeared to be fading and Jones came forward more frequently, taking advantage of the shift in momentum with sneaky counters up close. From then onwards, it was Jones' opportunity to use his experience. Seven years older and with double the amount of professional fights, he looked to be more comfortable and Anthony entered new territory.

To Anthony's credit, he bit down on his gum shield and made a real effort in the eighth round, working away with a mix of arm-punches, used to distract attention away from his harder overhands. Jones enjoyed the ninth round, the only adversity coming when Anthony again targeted the body, but it was controlled. Round 10 followed the same pattern and there was little to separate them at the final bell. The difference, however slight, was Jones' consistency and it managed to nullify Anthony's attempts to turn it back in his favour before the final bell.

Both sides could make a case for their boxer deserving the win – it was that close. The main controversy in this Welsh title fight wasn't who won; it was the margin of the official scoring that determined the new champion. It credited Anthony with just two of the 10 rounds. Richie Garner, who cornered Angelo Dragone less than an hour earlier, let his feelings known in the post-fight interview with S4C. The trainer and manager believed both of his boxers had been hard done-by. Despite the frustration, Anthony had performed well in his first major step up.

"Full respect to Morgan Jones. He suffered a heavy knockdown, he got up, he recovered and he boxed well behind the jab" said Garner to set up his more forthright complaint. "But we knew Martin Williams is the type of referee who scores for aggression and pressing the fight. I thought we done enough to win, I'm not going home happy with the decision. I've got a 21-year-old boy here who, by the referee's decision, is going home shafted."

Naturally, Jones disagreed and had his own interpretation of events. The victor did offer his gracious sympathies to Anthony, though. Jones recognised the similarities between their respective situations, having been in Anthony's shoes not so long ago. They have sparred together in the past and within Jones' empathy was a belief that the win will look better in the future when Anthony goes on to other achievements.

He said: "I knew I won the fight, I knew deep in my heart I won. Really speaking, to me, that's all that matters. Whatever decision is given, it doesn't matter to me. I knew I won that fight.

"I had already taken two losses. I knew how it felt to lose your unbeaten record. I knew that, y'know? At that last bell, my heart was really with Jake. I know what it feels like. In my head, I felt bad for him and I hope he comes back stronger.

"If Jake keeps sticking at it and stays in the game, he's going to do a lot of good things. The hardest thing in pro boxing is staying active. If he keeps fighting and people are willing to fight him, he's going to surprise a lot of people."

Photo: Sacha Wiener

DIXON GIVEN BIRTHDAY BRUISES AS HE SHREDS RING RUST
Friday 13 September 2019

Dark blue bruises didn't dampen the mood of Mountain Ash's Tony Dixon (12-2, 3KO), who marked his birthday with a bumpy 97-94 win against Devon's Faheem Khan (14-11-2, 1KO).

"It wasn't a normal birthday but it was a good night," said the 'Welsh Terrier' – a nickname that acknowledged both his status as a two weight champion of his country and his love of hunting. "It was a bit mental, everyone kind of forgot about my birthday!"

Dixon hadn't been seen in the ring since edging out Kieran Gething in a Fight of the Year contender for the Welsh welterweight title, remaining inactive for 11 months following the win in 2018. Promoter Sanigar Events, who also handled management duties, welcomed Dixon's return to action at Swansea's LC2 and broadcaster S4C showed the fight against Khan on taped delay.

From the outset, Dixon circled to his left in an attempt to negate the challenge of Khan's southpaw stance. It manoeuvred Khan to the edges of the ring, where Dixon was able to commit to wide hooks. However, the visitor had his own success in the early exchanges. Crafty head clashes and cute crosses left Dixon with a badly swollen eye and he was well aware of the fight on his hands by the end of the second round.

"I think they [the head clashes] were on accident but it was a lot of times. They smashed me straight in the eyes," winced Dixon afterwards. "I couldn't see out of one eye. All the way through [the fight], I could hardly see. My eye was always funny anyway, so it kind of done me a favour.

"I felt a bit ring rusty. I know he was a southpaw. A slippery, awkward guy. He's a good, awkward fighter. They'd done their homework on me and he didn't do bad, in all fairness to him."

Dixon was clumsily bundled over by a right hook in the third round and he quickly rose to dispute referee Reece Carter's instant count, adamant he'd tripped to the canvas. The response in the following rounds saw a full throttle attack and it unsettled Khan, who looked to hastily escape from the pressure.

"I genuinely slipped. He didn't even touch me. I said to him [the referee], 'are you serious?' He just looked at me and started counting anyway. I jumped back and tripped over my own foot, he wasn't even near me," Dixon insisted.

"I thought to myself, 'I need to make that up.' So, it did me a favour… even though it didn't. It got a bit of fire back in me. I liked the boy, he was too nice to me to start off and I couldn't get any aggression into me. So, I thought I better up my game or the fight was gonna go the other way."

The 27-year-old Welshman had established momentum by the middle rounds and Khan's replies became more infrequent. Dixon pressed on, giving Khan no respite and the pattern was repeated in the closing rounds. A high pace was set and Dixon, encouraged by coach Paul Paveltish, always had the first and last say.

They veered from corner to corner and energy levels appeared to deplete, until Dixon summoned the strength for one last surge of stamina. He launched a huge onslaught in the 10th and final round and the referee would've been justified in halting the action. Khan withstood the punches until the final bell. As the visitor regained his breath, Dixon congratulated him on playing his part in a tougher than expected return to the ring.

He said: "To be honest, definitely he [the referee] should've stopped that. It was a lot of punishment and he [Khan] done well to stay on his feet. I'll give him that, credit where it's due."

The fight served as an eliminator for the Commonwealth title held by Swansea's Chris Jenkins, a friend of Dixon who was atop the domestic scene. It was possible their paths could cross in the future and Dixon was lukewarm to the idea of fighting his friend, even with the British title on the line.

"If it come down to it, obviously the money would have to be good. Me and Chris are good friends and hopefully it never comes to it but if it does, it does," he said, with a hint of regret.

"Me and Chris go way back. We used to spar all the time; we've done loads of rounds together. He knows what I'm like and I know what he's like. It's going to be one of them fights, 'who does it on the night.'

"He's a good mate. I'd never slag him off and I don't think he'd slag me off in that type of way, y'know. We are genuinely friends but what can you do about it?"

Photo: Sacha Wiener

SIX STRAIGHTFORWARD WINS ON THE SANIGAR EVENTS UNDERCARD
Friday 13 September 2019

The show in Swansea was supported by six of Welsh boxing's up and comers, all triumphing amidst little resistance from tough but unambitious journeymen.

It was typical of the matchmaking found on the UK's small hall scene, accepted by observers given the budgets available. Promoters at grass roots levels almost exclusively rely on ticket sales to fund their shows. Local fans usually forgive boxers for facing such light opposition in the early stages of their careers and all parties understand that if the prospects proceed then sterner tests await in the future. For now, they're afforded time in their comfort zone to ensure crucial and intangible experience is gained.

Ystrad Rhondda's Jordan Withers (1-0) debuted with a straightforward points win against Portsmouth's Liam Griffiths (5-84-1), scored 40-36 by referee Reece Carter. The middleweight eased his way into action, edging forward with his hands floating by his waist. Griffiths never took the bait and was happy to retreat, allowing Withers the room to chip away throughout the duration. Withers' most impressive work came when he visited the body, often sinking in uppercuts when Griffiths tucked up on the ropes and the maiden win never looked in danger. Time spent training in America with Lee Selby was put to good use.

Risca's rangy welterweight Jake Tinklin (4-0) made use of his size advantage over Lee Hallett (1-20) to collect a 40-37 points win over four rounds. Often working from long distance, Tinklin looked to land straight shots and he dictated the pace in the first round. Hallett showed some spirit in the second round, winging away with wild hooks when Tinklin held his feet for too long. Tinklin returned to the plan in the next sessions, seizing centre ring for long periods and forcing Hallett to the edges of the ring. Hallett remained ambitious until the end, but drew warning from referee Chris Jones for a low blow. It was a busy weekend for Tinklin's trainer Gavin Rees, who headed for London straight away afterwards for Kody Davies' British title eliminator.

Bridgend's sharp-shooting switch-hitter Robbie Vernon (4-0, 2KO) continued his unbeaten run and worked his way to a 40-36 decision win against Chris Adaway (9-59-4, 1KO). The super-lightweight was straight down to business and never reacted to Adaway's taunts. Vernon kept his shape throughout, even when unloading a powerful and sustained two-fisted flurry in the second round. The 24-year-old landed eye-catching single shots in the fourth round and persuaded Adaway to retreat until the final bell

Ruthin's super-welterweight Sion Yaxley (3-0) stayed patient and boxed neatly to defeat Danny Little (8-61-2, 1KO), earning a clear-cut 40-36 distance win. The well-balanced 23-year-old got closer throughout the four rounder and found the room to land a steady stream of jabs and right crosses. Yaxley threw occasional right hands to the body and Little, opting to circle away, was wise to the attacks. Little rarely threatened Yaxley, who remained compact when anything speculative came his way.

Speedy super-bantamweight Joshua John (1-0) debuted with a quick-fisted win over the visiting Jose Aguilar (16-64-5, 6KO), judged to be 40-36. The standout amateur was way too quick, darting in and out of range before Aguilar had a chance to get to grips with him. It pleased a large contingent from Port Talbot.

Cardiff's Lloyd Germain (1-0) closed the show with a controlled decision against Torquay's Adam Bannister (1-9) and took another 40-36 win. The 29-year-old super-welterweight was made to wait all night for his fight, climbing through the ropes at 11:30pm, but nothing about his performance indicated he was affected. Instead, Germain closed Bannister down and landed when the visitor tried to change direction to bring the show to a close.

Photo: Liam Hartery

DROPPED DAVIES BOUNCES BACK TO BEAT CHELLI
Saturday 14 September 2019

Pontllanfraith's light-heavyweight Kody Davies (10-0, 3KO) was knocked down for the first time and had to rally back to win against Zak Chelli (7-1, 3KO) in a battle of unbeaten prospects.

After 10 tense and tactical rounds, three English judges favoured Davies with unanimous 96-94, 96-93, 97-92 scorecards at London's iconic York Hall. Davies' appearance in the British title eliminator came in the away corner and the 25-year-old's recovery against hometowner Chelli must have impressed Queensberry Promotions' Frank Warren.

The duo waited patiently in the opener until Davies came forward with more intent in the second round. A straight left power punch forced Chelli into the corner and troubled awaited as Davies rushed in with another attack. Chelli, a recent Southern Area champion at the weight below, uncorked a cracking uppercut that Davies didn't see coming. The Welshman sunk to the floor, quickly rising to audaciously protest the referee's count. It was worth a go.

"I got tagged early on," said Davies to the BT Sport commentary team. "I pretended I tripped over, but I didn't trip over. I got caught and I thought I needed to change something."

Davies, equipped with a newfound respect for Chelli's power, still didn't shy away from exchanges in the third and fourth rounds. Instead, he just retained his discipline when committing to attacks. Both boxers attempted to trigger the other and Davies did it better, using feints to gain position on the front foot. Davies was clearly effective in the fifth round and he kept a twitchy Chelli reversing into the uncertainty of no man's land. Speedy flurries occupied Chelli's attention and Davies dropped long left crosses into the exchanges to make a deeper dent in his opponents' defence.

Appearing to have gotten a measure of Chelli's extra-wide stance, Davies frequently managed to dash into range and make his notable size advantage count. His enthusiasm seemed to sap Chelli's energy at the halfway mark. Trainer Gavin Rees, a former domestic and world champion, beckoned Davies on and Chelli's attempts to hold for a rest drew attention from referee

Ian John Lewis. Meanwhile, mentor and legend Joe Calzaghe literally waved his encouragement from ringside.

Davies made sure he didn't overcommit again and another long left cross badly stunned Chelli, who took advantage of a borderline low blow to gain a one-minute break during the sixth round. From this point on, Davies marched forward with wave after wave of controlled attacks. The momentum was set and all Davies had to do was avoid Chelli's rationed pot shots on his way in.

The eighth round was quieter and Davies even took the time to ask Chelli to engage, a sign that the flow of the fight wouldn't shift again. Perhaps Davies wondered if Chelli was saving his energy for a big finish but it was easily handled when it came, albeit leading to a handful of messy clinches in the final round. The victory against Chelli should've put Davies in line to contest the British title, which was expected to be vacated by 2016 Olympic medallist Joshua Buatsi.

"The options are all open at super-middleweight and light-heavyweight," smiled Davies at ringside with interviewer Ronald McIntosh.

"I've proven myself at super-middleweight already. I've sparred with some of the best in the world and put one of them on their backside [rumoured to be WBA champion Callum Smith], so I know I can mix it there.

"I could see Zak fading and it takes something mentally to see when somebody is on the fade," he said in assessment of the performance. "I knew I was going to catch him sooner or later. I probably messed around a little bit too much, but that's just what I do."

Prevailing in a battle of unbeaten prospects was an important step for Davies, though he kept perspective by kissing his glove and touching the top of his trunks shortly after the scorecards were announced. 'Jade' was the word adorned in teal sequins on Davies' waistband. It was a tribute his older sister, who passed away suddenly and unexpectedly months earlier. Davies now dedicated his boxing career to Jade's memory, which was kept alive by her brother's strength in the spotlight.

Photo: Huw Fairclough

PRIORITY BOXING PLANT A FLAG IN THE CAPITAL
Friday 20 September 2019

Mo Prior's Priority Boxing returned to Welsh soil for a seven-fight show and planted a flag in the capital city. The Vale Sports Arena were keen to host shows on a regular basis and Priority Boxing's first visit of the season saw another crop of Welsh talents develop in the early stages of their professional careers.

The show was topped by the late addition of Ireland's John Joe Nevin (13-0, 4KO). Now trained by Jim McDonnell, Nevin negotiated his way past Jordan Ellison (11-24-1, 1KO) in an uneventful eight rounder scored 80-73. The 30-year-old was an unexpected addition to the number of Olympic finalists to appear in Cardiff in recent years, following; Anthony Joshua, Alexander Povetkin, Guillermo Rigondeaux, Katie Taylor and Daniyar Yeleussinov.

Cardiff's Maredudd Thomas (9-0, 2KO) kicked the show off with a controlled 59-55 decision against London's Lee Hallett (1-21) over six one-sided rounds. The chiselled welterweight cut an imposing figure from the start. Thomas stalked Hallett and tracked him down with a stream of solid jabs. A hurtful uppercut and a chopping left hook were enough to convince Hallett to clinch for the remainder of the opening round. There were tasty exchanges to start the second round until Thomas' power punches again discouraged Hallett. Thomas elected to counterpunch on the front foot in the third and fourth rounds, planting shots to Hallet's midsection when the visitor overextended and it caused him to visibly wince. Hallett was cornered in the fifth and sixth rounds, and he remained smart enough to avoid an early finish. Promisingly, there was still more to come from Thomas. It was an impressive performance, especially considering Hallett gave a good account of himself against Risca's Jake Tinklin a week earlier.

Newport's Craig Woodruff (8-5, 2KO) looked red-hot as he punished Lester Cantillano (4-32, 3KO) over four rounds to collect a 40-35 scorecard. The former Welsh lightweight champion made a major impression in the opening exchange and the win never looked in danger. Woodruff used his long levers to whip in an assortment of wide hooks that were often out of Cantillano's eye line right up to the moment they landed. He paid particular attention to the body in the second round and Cantillano clearly wilted. A left hook almost sent Cantillano flying out of the ring at the end of the session and referee Reece Carter correctly ruled a knockdown when the ropes prevented the tumble. Cantillano occasionally attacked in the third and fourth rounds. The bravery was rewarded when the Nicaraguan heard the final bell.

Woodruff was back to winning ways in his first fight since Welsh title disappointment against super-lightweight champion Kieran Gething at the very same venue three months earlier.

Rhoose's super-welterweight Jay Munn (1-0) debuted with a shutout 40-36 win against Blackwood's Paul Ducie (0-13). Composure was needed in the first round as Munn pressed and Ducie instantly withdrew, checking in at all corners of the ring. The southpaw opponent stayed away from danger until Munn buzzed him with a short straight right. Munn briefly switched to the southpaw stance in the second round and it opened the angle for left cross, sparking 'Rhoose rhino' chants from his following. A left uppercut had the same effect in the third round, and it was all going Munn's way until the fourth round followed a different script. With the win all but confirmed, Munn backed off and Ducie occupied the vacant space. That session meant Ducie had a reason to fondly remember his first professional fight in his home country, even if he wasn't awarded it on the scorecard.

Rhoose's Lance Cooksey (11-0, 2KO) banked every round against Edwin Tellez (12-56-5, 6KO) to earn an easy 60-54 decision victory. The super-featherweight began busily, always looking to close the gap and throw bursts of quick combos. Tellez didn't reflect the same output but he shared a similar stance and both worked away with short hooks behind their compact guards. Cooksey became more direct in the third round and enjoyed more success. He often finished his attacks with left hooks to the body, constantly keeping Tellez turning and not allowing him to get set. Cooksey forced the pace in the fourth round and his authority was never in jeopardy. The fifth and sixth rounds were fought at a less frantic speed. Cooksey turned the screw with more guile, connecting long rights around Tellez' defence. It was time to step up.

Tonypandy's Rhys Edwards (7-0, 2KO) visited the sixth round for the first time as a professional, punching out a 60-54 decision win against the durable Jose Aguilar (16-66-5, 6KO). The 19-year-old prospect looked like a special talent since turning professional and it was no different on this night. Edwards was a box of tricks in the opening round, mixing power-punches with crafty pivots and uppercuts on the inside. Aguilar appeared increasingly angry with Edwards' boldness and responded with wild replies. The sharp shooting talent accelerated, launching and landing double left hooks on a number of occasions. When Aguilar expected the left hooks, right hooks were then introduced and the defending visitor was always kept guessing. Edwards walked Aguilar down in the third round, zipping into the firing line to uncork crunching blows to the body. Aguilar tried to respond and often hit fresh air as the target swayed and ducked out of the way. The Gary Lockett-trained operator went through the gears in the fourth round to unsettle Aguilar with his variety. The fifth and sixth rounds were quieter as Edwards spent more time picking his punches. Aguilar, knowing his place, was grateful for the rest and didn't look to claw any of the rounds back. The Welshman jabbed more, poking it between Aguilar's arms to trigger openings and comfortably cruised home.

Cardiff's welterweight Jamie JJ Evans (9-0) was all business as he closed the show with a six round decision win against Geiboord Omier (4-44-1, 3KO), judged to be 60-54. The methodical southpaw feinted and established his jab early. Omier retreated and looked uncomfortable as Evans stalked with straights that frequently found the target. Evans targeted the body in the second round and Omier responded by holding when they came close together. Soon shortening his work, Evans drilled more body shots to Omier's unbalanced torso and the visitor's complaints of low blows didn't register with referee Chris Jones.

The length of Evans' combinations increased in the third round. The 10-time Welsh amateur champion marched Omier around the ring with arching left hands and scored with uppercuts when they stood close. The flow of the fight remained in the fourth, fifth and sixth rounds. Omier was fortunate not to receive warnings for his negative tactics. On the other hand, it was Evans' most positive performance since turning professional three years ago and he was another who looked ready to step up to riskier matchups.

Photo: Liam Hartery

THUNDER THORLEY RETURNS TO RESTART CAREER
Friday 27 September 2019

Cardiff's new look Nathan Thorley (13-0, 6KO) returned from an extended absence to restart his career in a new weight division. 26-year-old 'Thunder' recorded a wide 60-54 decision over Lithuania's Remigijus Ziausys (20-107-5, 10KO) at London's York Hall to mark the start of a new chapter.

Having won the Welsh light-heavyweight title in 2017, Thorley headed north to campaign at cruiserweight for the foreseeable future. The categories are separated by 25lbs – the largest gap in boxing's laddered structure. Thorley's six-foot four-inch frame outgrew the 175lbs limit during an 11 month period of inactivity, a baron spell impacted by a separation from management Sanigar Events. The conclusion of a BBBoC hearing in June meant Thorley was free to move on and he soon signed with London-based manager Mo Prior.

"I done things no boxer should ever have to do," said Thorley of his time struggling with the scales. "I can't say I was eating well, I was eating like a rabbit really. I was eating next to nothing, training two or three times a day, running a ridiculous amount of miles and jumping in saunas before weigh-ins. It was never, ever good for me.

"I'm a different fighter. I can now eat more, I'm pumping more fluids in, whereas I wasn't drinking or hardly eating. I've got more energy, I feel fitter, stronger. My punch resistance is a lot better. It's crazy how much I feel better. It's the biggest jump in boxing, it's nearly two stone."

Thorley comfortably negotiated his way through the action with Ziausys and plenty was left in the locker. Most impressively, his movement deducted Ziausys to being a passive plodder and the visitor was too basic when he tried to use his 10lb weight advantage. Thorley, owner of the longest reach in Welsh boxing, put his assets to use by scoring right crosses. The favoured right hand seemed speedier against bigger, slower opposition and indicated it could be a potent weapon in new territory at cruiserweight.

Ziausys' arms were tied up when he got close and the fight showed no signs of ending early. His durability had already been proven in the past, going the distance with the likes of world-class heavyweight Dillian Whyte in 2011. Initially, Thorley was set to appear on the show in Cardiff a week ago. Those plans went askew when a scheduled foreign opponent failed to board the plane and the replacement date was rapidly arranged. Whatever the circumstances, he was just happy to be back under the lights.

"I was over the moon when I was able to fight again," beamed Thorley. "There's no feeling like it. Honestly, it was the best feeling in the world.

"Halfway through the fight, I started smiling and I was just happy to be back in the ring. I'm in this sport to make a name for myself, y'know. Money doesn't bother me, I just want to fight. I just want to get in, take shots, give shots and put on entertainment for people."

Coach Gary Lockett had spent hundreds of hours in the gym with Thorley but it only translated to one fight due to the inactivity. The latest instalment of disruption meant corner duties had to be delegated. Lockett had already committed to be with Abertillery's Jack Shore in Copenhagen as the mixed martial artist [MMA] made a brutally successful debut with the world-leading Ultimate Fighting Championship [UFC] promotion. Shore, who won a Welsh amateur novice title in 2013, kept his 'striking' sharp by working with Lockett.

With a renewed vigour, Thorley was hopeful his own nights against championship opposition were on the horizon. The domestic scene at cruiserweight was bursting with a new generation of young and hungry contenders and Thorley was planning to make room for a Welshman.

"I've gone from fighting some of the best in the world as an amateur to fighting nobodies as a pro, so I think it's time to make my dreams a reality and get in with the best fighters in Britain."

Photo: Sacha Wiener

SELBY SHINES… AND THEN SURVIVES SERIOUS SCARE
Saturday 28 September 2019

Two fights in a fortnight almost caught up with Barry's Andrew Selby (13-1, 7KO) as he experienced the full spectrum of drama on offer in a boxing ring.

First up, Selby bamboozled Worawatchai Boonian (14-23-2, 13KO) in less than a round on a Mack The Knife [MTK] Global glamour night in Dubai. The flyweight swarmed all over his Thai opponent and sent him to the canvas twice before it was sensibly waved off.

Two weeks later, it was Selby's turn to visit the floor twice and a supposedly routine outing against Tanzania's Fadhili Majiha (24-14-4, 11KO) called on all of his resolve over eight rounds in Newcastle. Referee Darren Maxwell favoured Selby via a razor thin 76-74 scorecard to ensure the comeback continued. Selby was still in the rebuilding stage, having lost a WBC world title eliminator to Julio Cesar Martinez in Mexico six months earlier. Plenty had changed since then.

The loss prompted Selby to sever ties with trainer Tony Borg and management Sanigar Events. Moving on, he linked up with former Team GB teammate Daniel Chapman as his new trainer and signed an advisory deal with MTK Global. The new team was supposed to provide structure and activity for Selby to help him to go back to boxing basics and overcome the loss to Martinez. It also aimed to aid his recovery from a dark place in his private life, a place that included addiction, legal problems and the unexpected death of his mother.

Selby, a 2016 Olympian and widely regarded as the best Welsh amateur boxer of all time, had long been known as one of the best movers in British boxing. The sight of him on the floor, sent there by a flush power punch in the first round, was surprising to everyone except Majiha. The African planted a right cross just as Selby crossed his feet and it sent him crashing to the neutral corner. Selby even had to take a knee before rising, just to be sure he was on steady legs. Pure grit and toughness were needed to survive, and Selby appeared to recover by the next session.

From rounds two to five, Selby's typically smooth skills were put to use – pivots, dips and speedy tricks kept him clear of danger. He scored with counters when Majiha tried too hard, the only issue was that the Welshman's punches couldn't deter Majiha from coming forward again and again. Majiha made a more concerning breakthrough in the sixth round. Selby was staggered by another right hand and he was unable to escape a sustained attack. His balance was betrayed by his legs and he was floored for a second time, this time stumbling southwards.

The final two rounds called on Selby's bravery and they still needed to be won. It led to anxious exchanges and both boxers staked a claim with their wildly contrasting skillsets. Selby's backers would have been concerned with the performance and his critics questioned if his best days were in the past.

Cardiff's Barry Jones, a former WBO super-featherweight champion, scored it as a draw in his co-commentary role for ESPN+ and iFL TV. Selby was equally sincere in his post-fight assessment.

"It was a very, very tough opponent," opened the 30-year-old to ringside interviewer Alex Steedman. "I can say now, I didn't think he hit hard but you'd think I was lying because he dropped me twice. They were big shots but I recovered well, I wasn't hurt, just hit flush on the button and maybe I over trained. I don't know. That was a five out of 10 today, I'm thankful for the win.

"I just felt like every bit of energy was sapped out of me but no excuses. I've been training like a maniac. Maybe we'll have to have a week off because I didn't have no time off.

"People hide behind their keypads to say I was shit… I was shit, excuse my language. I was terrible but I was a good terrible because I won. This guy is a tough man. You can't box amazing on every single fight.

"I'll tell you how I want it, because now they can't hide from me. Jay Harris, you've seen how shit I was, so when you fight [Paddy] Barnes, I want the winner for the European title. If you can't beat me like that, then you want to quit yourself."

Selby, the British champion who was yet to defend his Lonsdale belt after winning it three years ago, had sent a challenge to Swansea's Jay Harris. As it happened, the reigning Commonwealth and European champion was in hunting season for former amateur stars.

LAST MINUTE DISRUPTION DOESN'T RUFFLE ROBINSON
Friday 4 October 2019

Cardiff's featherweight Jacob Robinson (7-0, 2KO) earned every round to fend off Sean Davis (14-7) and end a week of last-minute chopping and changing.

Originally, Robinson was supposed to fight in his home city on the Priority Boxing show a fortnight earlier. However, the matchmakers came up short and his management team MTK Global stepped in to ensure a training camp wouldn't go to waste. They matched Robinson with Sheffield's Razaq Najib and they were due to meet on the undercard of the Golden Contract tournament. However, Najib was called up as a replacement for the tournament, which included seven other quality operators. A lucrative deal awaited whoever prevailed through the competition's three stages.

Robinson was then matched with Davis, who accepted the fight on 24 hours' notice. Davis marked a significant step up for Robinson and boasted an English title in his trophy cabinet, albeit coming at the lower division of super-bantamweight. Robinson's maiden eight rounder was scored 80-72 by referee Jeff Hinds and streamed on Sky Sports' social media channels.

'Baby Jake' smoothly eased into action. He tried to activate a response from Davies but any chances to counter and capitalise were few and far between in the following rounds. Robinson remained in his lower gears for the most part and the pace didn't accelerate far beyond the speed limit.

A steady stream of singles landed for Robinson, enough to win every round from the safety of his comfort zone. Davis appeared content to go the distance – an approach possibly justified by his acceptance of the fight on late notice. Matt Macklin, as part of the Sky Sports commentary team, was forthright in his analysis. The world title challenger spotted areas for Robinson to work on and remained constructive with his criticism.

"Robinson is always in control but I'd like to see a little bit more adventure, more combinations," summarised Macklin during the final round. "It's a fight that's never really caught fire. Robinson has always been in control, he's comfortable. Davis seems happy enough to play his part and get through the rounds; he's taken it at short notice.

"As the house fighter and prospect, the onus is on Robinson really to make the fight, take the initiative and take the fight to Davis. Davis will be happy when he hears the final bell, he'll think [the] job [is] done.

"I don't want to be too critical of Robinson. He's only had six fights and it's an eight rounder, Davis is certainly an experienced opponent. So, he [Robinson] is probably happy just to bag the eight rounds and get the experience but moving forward, this is something they'll want to look back on and think about putting the foot to the floor a bit quicker."

It was worth noting that Robinson only had 22 amateur fights and this was his first professional fight outside of his home country. There was plenty of experience still to gain.

Photo: Liam Hartery

WORLD CHAMPIONSHIP MEDAL ESCAPES ECCLES' REACH IN RUSSIA
Wednesday 9 October 2019

Caldicot's Rosie Eccles went further than her nearest rival at the World Championships but a medal escaped the amateur puncher.

The 23-year-old was locked in a two-horse race for Team GB's welterweight spot at the 2020 Olympic Games and managed to take a slight step ahead of England's Sandy Ryan. After Ryan was surprisingly eliminated in the first round, University of South Wales graduate Eccles reached the second round of the tournament in Ulan-Ude, eastern Siberia. It was the latest twist in the tussle for a place on the plane to Tokyo for the 29th summer Olympic Games.

Earlier in the rivalry, Eccles was narrowly out-pointed by Ryan in the 2018 Commonwealth Games final but recovered to flip the result in more convincing fashion at the 2019 European Championships quarter-finals in August. When in Wales, Eccles trained with Lyndon James at Pontypool ABC. However, 'Right Hand' Rosie usually spent her weekdays training right alongside Ryan in Sheffield with Team GB at the English Institute of Sport. They fought for favour with the Team GB squad selectors and remained impressively sporting during the high-stakes rivalry.

The 11th edition of the Women's World Championships started well for Eccles. All five judges favoured her efforts and awarded every round in a unanimous decision against Argentina's Lucia Perez. Eccles pushed the pace from the first to last bell and even forced a 10-8 round with two of the scoring officials.

Eccles was back in the ring three days later and faced China's world class Liu Yang. Attacking in her typically aggressive manner, Eccles appeared stronger and gave Yang a standing eight count at the end of the second round. Expectation increased but Yang made the other rounds close enough to state her case. Eccles raised her arms in celebration when the fight ended but she was denied a big win when the result was officially announced. All five judges favoured Yang in a unanimous decision.

"So, yesterday my World Championships sadly came to an end. It was so close but not the result we wanted against China. The performance was there against world-class opposition," said Eccles in reaction on social media. "I know I'm not far away. My dream is to be an Olympian, an Olympic medallist, gold medallist. Nothing is ever straightforward but despite not coming home world champion, the dream feels so possible. [I've] just got to keep chipping away and the titles will come. My time is coming."

The result enabled Yang to progress all the way to the final. The Chinese boxer earned a silver medal and the last day of the tournament was also the stage for Eccles' Welsh teammate to make history.

HARRIS BREAKS DOWN BARNES IN BELFAST WITH WORLD LEVEL IN HIS SIGHTS
Friday 11 October 2019

Swansea's Jay Harris (17-0, 9KO) signalled his stardom by ending the career of Ireland's Paddy Barnes (6-3, 1KO) in four storming rounds and heading to world level.

'The Leprechaun' was an apt nickname for Belfast's pint-sized puncher Barnes, a red-head standing at just five foot four inches tall. The only feature of a mythical Irish fairy missing for the flyweight was the most important ingredient - a bit of luck. It had seemingly deserted 32-year-old Barnes since he ended a stellar amateur career to join the paid code in 2016. Though undoubtedly well-paid, the treble-Olympian struggled to impress in most of his professional outings and failed to recreate the form that captured medals at most of the major international amateur tournaments.

Before fighting Harris, there were six victories against a crop of unambitious opponents and two reverses on Barnes' ledger. That skid included a fourth round stoppage loss in a dubiously deserved shot at then-WBC world champion Cristofer Rosales, and a bruising decision defeat to American club fighter Oscar Mojica in New York on St Patrick's Day. For those reasons, the European Boxing Union [EBU] refused to sanction a challenge to Harris, their reigning champion. It was an understandable decision for the EBU given Barnes' form, which included just one win in 14 months and that sole triumph came against a Nicaraguan journeyman.

Belt collecting was a hereditary habit for the Harris family, headed by former Welsh and British featherweight champion Peter Harris. However, there was no significant signing fee when his son Jay turned professional in 2013, instead he walked away with just £140 in his pocket. The debut was practically a loss-making exercise once he shelved out for his first set of medicals and license fees. Pontyclun-based manager Gary Lockett persisted to provide opportunities for Harris, whilst Peter handled the bulk of training in the gym. Harris managed to stop half of his opponents inside the distance and he picked up the Commonwealth title with a well-earned decision against Cameroon's Olympian Thomas Essomba in 2017. Oddly, Hall of Fame promoter Frank Warren lost interest immediately afterwards and Harris was condemned to boxing's wastelands, reappearing on the small hall scene to stay relevant.

Broken promises were forgotten about when Harris was snapped up by the increasingly influential MTK Global in early 2019. The Dubai-based outfit was initially co-founded by former boxer Matt Macklin in 2012 and it soon boasted a plethora of world-class talent, including Tyson Fury and Carl Frampton. Harris was given a routine outing against Brett Fidoe on MTK Global's first show on Welsh soil in March, where he produced a below par performance, and he then received the opportunity to headline their second show. Spain's recent world title challenger Angel Moreno provided little threat as Harris ran away with a wide unanimous decision and the blue EBU belt at the height of summer to set up the Barnes fight.

MTK Global's initial investment was rewarded and they turned attention to the world scene. The absence of European honours prompted the inclusion of the International Boxing Federation's [IBF] Inter-Continental title. Harris was ranked sixth by the sanctioning body, whose South African champion Moruti Mthalane was also in the MTK Global stable alongside Barnes. With a stake in a lot of relevant flyweights, MTK Global brought major exposure to the lighter weight classes by streaming shows live on YouTube channel iFL TV and ESPN+ in America. It was a far cry from the small hall shows Harris had appeared on as recently as 11 months earlier and he flew to Belfast feeling fortunate.

The pre-fight talk remained respectful; both smiled awkwardly during face-offs for the cameras and they agreed on most points, including opinions on the 12 rounds of sparring they'd previously shared. Barnes' more venomous verbal jabs were scored online, where he often went viral with comedic quips to creditors and critics alike. However, Harris was spared and the most recent victim was heavyweight legend Lennox Lewis. The latest argument was hardly ideal preparation the night before a crucial fight in Barnes' career.

Although on away soil, Harris instantly looked at home. He recreated a scene similar to Swansea city centre with his own version of a one-way traffic system. Straight rights and screw shots stiffened a wide-eyed Barnes and he squeezed his guard to endure the attacks. Barnes attempted his own quick salvos, but they lacked the power to damage Harris. Instead, Harris marched forward with more blows and he retained an ice-cold composure. Both stood in the pocket in the second round. The difference wasn't just Harris' power but his ring smarts, too. An old school cross-arm stance enabled him to lean backwards away from Barnes' work, before he returned with heavy replies.

Barnes began the third round brightly, firing a sustained burst of short hooks to head and body. Not all of them got through but Harris was now cut above his right eye. Harris responded quickly and punished Barnes for his ambition; rocking his head back and issuing a call to war. Barnes, now bloodied himself, accepted the challenge and toe-to-toe exchanges entertained the sold-out Ulster Hall in a round of the year contender. However, whilst Barnes was revving his engine to the max, Harris looked like he was just starting to get going.

The breakthrough came with a left hook to the body. It folded the brave Barnes who rolled on the floor and an equally brutal follow up attack, consisting of around a dozen unanswered punches, made for uncomfortable viewing. Barnes' corner, led by Danny Vaughan, would've been justified in waving a white towel but they resisted. There was a clear difference in size and Harris towered above Barnes. Many, even Harris' own team, were surprised to learn that the Welshman was only three pounds over the eight stone limit at the IBF's check weigh-in on the morning of the fight.

Harris reintroduced his right hand in the fourth round and he couldn't miss the target. Barnes remained busy but his attempts were now desperate and inaccurate. It presented openings for Harris to pick his shots – and he did. Another left hook to the body returned Barnes to the floor and this time, he wasn't getting up. A statement was made, and it sent 40 travelling fans into delirious celebrations.

"He said it was going to be 'do or die.' He was coming to knock my head off but I give it back as good as I get it," Harris told commentator Alex Steedman at ringside. "I've never boxed in the Ulster Hall before ever but I got told what the atmosphere was going to be like and it didn't disappoint. It's absolutely electric in here."

Manager Gary Lockett was equally enthused: "We've been on a fantastic journey. Peter entrusted me with Jay's career from the start and we're finally there.

"We're working with MTK. We've got plans for the mandatory [Mohammed Obbadi], which could potentially double up as an IBF world title eliminator as well.

"It's a shame for Paddy, he's a lovely fella. Y'know, this is how boxers should treat each other. They should be respectful and it's been like that for the last few days. Well done to both."

Barnes slipped to 6-3, 1KO and grumbles of retirement sounded louder. Meanwhile, Harris extended his run to 17-0, 9KO and further cemented his rankings with all four sanctioning bodies – the IBF, World Boxing Council [WBC], World boxing Association [WBA] and World Boxing Organisation [WBO]. A bid to become world champion had become a real possibility.

Photo: Liam Hartery

PRICE CLAIMS WORLD CROWN TO CREATE HISTORY
Sunday 13 October 2019

Ystrad Mynach's Lauren Price left the ring with her head bowed, evidently disappointed at being pipped to the post by long-time Netherlands rival Nouchka Fontijn. Just 20 minutes later, the 25-year-old stood in complete contrast as Wales' first world amateur champion and forever a history maker.

Straight after the official announcement of a narrow 3-2 split decision loss, Welsh and Team GB officials met to quickly confer their options and organise immediate action. A decision was made to launch a daring appeal to overturn the result of the World Championships final in Ulan-Ude, eastern Siberia. 30-27, 30-27 and 29-28 scorecards had initially favoured Fontijn, whilst Price earned two 29-28 tallies from the five judges. The International Boxing Association [AIBA] swiftly assembled a 'Bout Review Jury' to take another look at the debated second round. The jury, which consisted of three neutral officials, contradicted the original decision and controversially rescored it in favour of Price. The result was overturned – the ambitious appeal worked!

The unprecedented u-turn gave a gold medal to Price and placed her as an eternal entrant in Welsh sporting record books. Fontijn was standing at the podium, waiting for the delayed medal ceremony to start when she heard the news. Needless to say, the Dutch middleweight didn't stick around to receive a downgraded silver medal.

Rob McCracken, GB Boxing's Performance Director, said: "Lauren has been absolutely fantastic for the last two years and thoroughly deserves to be world champion. She has been getting better and better and winning the world championship is a fantastic reward for all of the hard work she has put in in the gym.

"This group of boxers is still relatively inexperienced, so to come to a tournament as tough as World Championships and leave with three medals is a fantastic performance. The boxers, coaches and all of the support staff should be very happy with what the team has achieved this last week.

"The squad is going in the right direction and the outlook is positive as we look towards the Olympic Games in less than a year."

This triumph marked the continuation of a remarkable run of form for Price. The latest addition to her trophy cabinet joined Commonwealth and European Games gold medals. That journey had seen her cross paths with Fontijn before, trading marginal wins and losses on a number of occasions. Most observers in Russia expected to see the top two middleweights meet again at the 2020 Olympics in Tokyo.

The threat posed by Price, who played over 50 times for Wales' national football team, was well-known to Fontijn. By this point, Price had mastered her crafty approach. The southpaw stance, speed of hand and elusive footwork formed a confusing conundrum for her opponents. The fights with Fontijn, a longer opponent who preferred to work at range, were always going to be cagey affairs but Price's slim win was a major confidence boost.

12 Welshmen had reigned as world champions, all of them exclusively in the professional code and mostly in eras when there was more than one avenue available. However, Price's achievement as an amateur was undoubtedly unique. It came in a format where medallists faced the best in their divisions. Tournament draws don't discriminate and paths to the top can't be picked as they can for professionals.

The World Championships were first held for male amateur boxers in 1974. A version for women was belatedly established 27 years later in 2001, but it had always been held separately to the male event. It provided the biggest platform for women until they were eventually accepted into the Olympics in 2012. The closest a male counterpart had come to coronation as world amateur champion was when Barry's flyweight Andrew Selby collected a silver medal in 2011. He was beaten in a razor-thin final by Russia's Misha Aloyan, who was favoured by a single point on the old computer-system scorecards. 12 years earlier, Kevin Evans was the first Welsh boxer to secure a medal in 1999. The heavyweight battled valiantly against Cuba's great Felix Savon in the semi-finals and Evans brought a bronze medal over the Loughor bridge to his home in Carmarthenshire.

Price's World Championship win wasn't just a big step forward for women's boxing in Wales, it was a big step for Welsh boxing as a whole. Repeating the feat at the 2020 Olympics would take it to another level of success and celebration.

DIXON DOES HIMSELF PROUD ON ITALIAN AWAY DAY
Friday 25 October 2019

A career best performance is usually a catalyst for celebration but there were conflicting feelings for Mountain Ash's Tony Dixon (12-3, 3KO) after an eventful away day outing.

The welterweight challenged the hard-hitting Maxim Prodan (18-0-1, 13KO) and found himself on the wrong end of a disputed split decision in Milan. 98-92, 97-93 and 94-96 scorecards favoured Prodan and the defeat meant Dixon was denied the IBF Inter-Continental title, as well as a top 15 rating with the organisation. Home advantage swung it in the favour of Prodan - a Romanian national, born in Ukraine and now based in Italy. It could've been different on neutral ground and whilst it wasn't wise to label the decision a robbery, Dixon's team had a fair case for disagreeing with two of the judges.

"Proud of Tony Dixon tonight," was the message from manager Jamie Sanigar. "Tony was on the wrong end of a split decision that I thought he won here in Milan. Tony proved he can mix it in this class and will come back stronger."

Dixon, since turning professional in 2012, always entertained and it was usually as a relentless aggressor. The sight of the 'Welsh Terrier' on the back foot and popping out a series of accurate jabs wasn't a familiar sight but that's what he did to frustrate Prodan from the opening bell – and he did it well. What made the performance even more surprising was its complete contrast to Dixon's style six weeks earlier against Faheem Khan. That rust-shedding rumble was very physical and saw Dixon leave damage around his eyes.

"I've just taken every fight that's come to me," he said of the quick turnaround, before elaborating on the change of tactics. "I've always been able to do it. We used to say, I can box and I can fight but 98% of the time… I fight. I'd rather fight, that's me, but when you've got a good fighter and another good fighter, there's only one place one of you is going and that's down or badly hurt.

"To be honest, I'd rather fight people like that. People said he had all these knockouts but to me, I can handle myself. I'm not bigging myself up but I'd rather those types of fights."

Under instruction from trainer Paul Paveltish, Dixon was ordered to jab, jab and jab again against Prodan. It saw the two-weight Welsh champion race to an early lead and he rarely missed with his jab in the early exchanges. 11 of Prodan's wins had come inside three rounds and he looked bewildered at Dixon's unwillingness to stand still. Prodan slowly followed Dixon around the borders of the ring and it was relatively easy pickings.

"I think he was shocked, I do," said Dixon. "He was walking to me, shaking his head all night. I could see he was getting frustrated and more frustrated. I kept whacking him and after the fight, we had to pee in a cup for a drug test and he was peeing blood. I was [peeing] clear."

Prodan's feet finally caught up with Dixon, who briefly leaned on the ropes, in the fourth round. The adopted Italian was prepared to take more risks but his work was inconsistent, evident when he became sloppy again in the fifth round. There was an argument that Prodan clawed back the deficit in the sixth and seven rounds. Crucially, the shorter man was effective in scheduling his better work at the end of rounds to ensure it was the final thing in the minds of the judges.

"He had a burst once or twice but a burst doesn't win you a fight. I could throw 10 punches at somebody in one round and think I've won but it doesn't work like that," said an unconvinced Dixon.

"After the sixth round when I was fighting in Italy, I thought I'd got him but I listened to my trainer and he said, 'keep doing what you're doing.'

"I was hitting him three times, straight in the face and he was just shaking his head at me. He walked me down and I kept doing the same thing."

Dixon looked to be feeling the pace at the end of the seventh round. However, he enjoyed a second wind in the eighth, moving behind his rejuvenated jab and both boxers recognised the need for a big finish. Prodan often fell short with his punches and Dixon took the opportunity to rally whenever his target was off balance, sure he'd done enough to secure the upset.

"I honestly thought they were gonna lift my hand. I genuinely did," said Dixon. "He didn't even put his hands up after the fight. He knew straight away [that] he'd lost. Pebbles [Paveltish] said to me, 'this ain't good, I think we're gonna get robbed now, boy.' I had my hands up and they said split decision.

"I boxed out of my skin. I could've done a bit more, I could've done some different stuff than jab and move, jab and move but he was a dangerous opponent. I thought to myself, 'I can hit him without getting hit, so I don't need to be getting into a fight.' I could've put a few more combos together and worked him that way but I think unless I knocked him out, I don't think I'd have ever got the win over there, anyway.

"In general, I would've given him three rounds and that's me being fair. I wouldn't give him any more, seriously. Honestly, if I thought I'd lost the fight, I'd hold my hands up and shake his hand and say, 'well done.' I lost to Ted Cheeseman and took it on the chin."

The contest wasn't televised for Welsh fans. It was instead broadcast to audiences in Europe and America on DAZN, a new online streaming platform. Eddie Hearn's Matchroom expanded into Italy and other new territories with funding from DAZN. Their record-breaking relationship was thought to be worth a billion dollars over an eight year period.

Dixon, a plasterer by trade, earned plenty of plaudits from onlookers, including commentators Nick Hailing and Alex Arthur. For that reason, matchmakers aren't likely to invite him back because of the danger he demonstrated, such is the cynical structure of the sport. Whatever would come next, Dixon wanted to stay at a competitive level, and he didn't think that included defending his Welsh titles at welterweight or super-welterweight.

"Time is ticking, I'm getting older," said Dixon, highlighting the reality of his situation. "This sport is hard and it's hard to keep yourself in the gym all the time. With kids, family and everything else going on with work, you can't afford to keep going on. Some people do it, but I couldn't afford to do boxing alone. I've got to work as well.

"I see it [the Welsh title] in the past. I was supposed to give one back in and I just don't see the point of fighting for them no more because there's no money in the Welsh [title], I'll be honest. It's absolutely rubbish.

"For a 10 round fight, it's absolutely poor. People would not believe what it's worth."

SELBY KEEPS WORLD TITLE HOPES ALIVE IN CLASH OF FORMER WORLD CHAMPIONS
Saturday 26 October 2019

Barry's Lee Selby (28-2, 9KO) kept his hopes of winning another world title alive with a vital win over Scottish legend Ricky Burns (43-8-1, 16KO).

The Welshman earned a majority decision courtesy of 115-115, 116-112 and 116-113 scorecards. It was Selby's first real test at lightweight, having lost his IBF world title two divisions lower at featherweight in May 2018.

Selby's rebuild on the Sky Box Office televised show came at the expense of former three-weight world champion Burns. Although likely to enjoy Eddie Hearn's home corner again, his time at the top table was probably at an end. For Selby, the plan for a return to world titles was on track.

"It was a good 12 round fight between two former world champions," summarised Selby. "It was a toss-up between Ricky Burns and Javier Fortuna. The Sanigars [management] and myself agreed the Burns fight for the simple reason the fight would be over here and he's more well-known. He's an established fighter in Britain, I'd get more credit beating him.

"I couldn't afford to lose. Although Ricky Burns is a great fighter, he was in the same position. That's how the fight was built up by Eddie Hearn and Matchroom. They built it up like it was a must win fight for both of us and whoever lost has to retire basically. It had a lot of pressure for both of us. I spoke to Ricky Burns afterwards and he said the same thing."

London's O2 Arena was a happy hunting ground for Selby. The docklands venue had been the scene for seven of his wins and a loss could've meant the end of his appearances on major shows. It was, unsurprisingly, difficult to enjoy the experience when the career consequences were so severe.

Selby said: "Half the time, you're thinking, 'why didn't I stay in school and get a proper education?' It's funny because after the weigh in, I always go to watch a movie with Chris Sanigar. He always says I should enjoy these times and 'what I'd give to be back in your shoes' and I'm thinking, 'bloody hell, I can't wait to be in your shoes!'"

The 32-year-old settled straight away. Selby circled Burns and unleashed a constant output. The movement was maintained in the early rounds and

Selby's work was more precise. Burns was punished when he missed and Selby, retaining better balance, repeatedly landed sharp straights before swiftly evading the replies.

After recognising the impressive start, Selby's ambition grew in the fourth round and he came forward more often. It led to more clinches and a frustrated Burns, inevitably, threw illegal rabbit punches to the back of Selby's head. The fouls were unaddressed by referee Bob Williams for the full 36 minutes. Burns grew bolder and tried to make it rough up close, becoming more blatant with his efforts to use his perceived size advantage. Selby redoubled his jab, it remained ever-present and irritated Burns, who lost his temper and threw blows after the bell to end the fifth round. The behaviour was out of character for the usually cool-headed veteran.

Burns landed some impressive straights on Selby's body but whenever they worked, Selby responded and was evidently ahead by the halfway mark. An accidental low blow and then a head clash temporarily halted the action, serving as the only interruption to the fight. Both occasions fuelled Burns' fire and he loaded up with a series of yelping power punches in an effort to stop the rot. Selby lost his shape amidst the hectic pressure and he threw a lot of his own single shots, a trait he's not normally associated with. Soon after, Selby's corner reminded him to return to his jab, the basic fundamentals of his success, and he managed to clips Burns enough to further consolidate the margin of his lead.

The energy levels of both regressed as they entered the championship rounds. Burns' relentless pursuit had reduced the deficit by a few rounds and Selby, footwork now slowing, finally met the bigger man head on in the middle of the ring. Overall, the tactics from trainer Tony Borg in the corner had been spot on. A clever approach had seen Selby consistently stick and move, craftily dipping out of sight when extended exchanges got risky. A big right cross landed from Burns in the closing seconds, though it was never going to be enough to unravel Selby's earlier work.

Newbridge's Joe Calzaghe remained the only Welsh boxer to rule the world at two weights. Supremacy at super-middleweight was followed with the lineal champion status at light-heavyweight. However, the Ring magazine belt isn't an officially recognised designation, technically leaving the door open for Selby to be the first Welsh boxer to win legitimate world titles in two divisions.

Selby's transition to the 135lb lightweight division was one of the most interesting sub-plots of the fight. Questions, from the outside looking in, had been answered. A sense of frailty was shed and his confidence soared throughout the fight. Selby was able to embrace muscle building training methods into his preparation and, for the first time in years, he looked strong enough to stand his ground.

Selby said: "I felt a lot stronger on my legs. Since I moved up two weights,

I've been able to do leg weights. That's something I've never been able to do throughout my career. In the fight, I could feel the difference and the benefit, I felt a lot stronger and sturdier on my feet.

"He [Burns] was an established lightweight champion and I was the bigger guy at the weigh-in and the night. It's still a struggle to make lightweight, it's not plain sailing and I can't eat what I want.

"It goes to show how much I took out of myself to make featherweight. Looking back, I don't know how I did it. I couldn't do it again, that's for sure."

The struggle to stay at featherweight had been an open secret, even dating back to Selby's British title reign. He confessed fears that one weight cut in particular, before a fight with Martin Lindsay in 2013, threatened his life. The featherweight limit of 126lbs was dangerous territory and yet he stayed there for another five years. What was once a size advantage had been reversed and instead worked against his weakening body.

"The night before the weigh-in, I thought I was going to die," said Selby, recalling the toughest weight cut of his career in Belfast, Northern Ireland. "I thought if I make it to the morning, I'm either retiring or moving up a weight. I was too disciplined to go to the bathroom sink and have a drink of water. I'd rather dry out and risk my health. That fight, I left the hotel [to go to the fight] at 10st 8lbs [148lbs], so I'd rehydrated 22lbs, which is massive for a featherweight.

"That's how much I took out of my body. Anything that went back in, I'd hold on to it. Any fluid, any food. There were times making featherweight, I weighed in and went for food and struggled to eat. I went back to my hotel room and near enough passed out, woke up a couple of hours later and then started eating."

Remarkably, domestic honours still came relatively easily but by the time he was world champion, the weight was clearly affecting his performances. The decision to stay at the 126lb limit for six fights after masterfully dethroning Evgeny Gradovich in 2015 was like walking a tightrope – there was no margin for error. Selby's reluctance to vacate the IBF title made him vulnerable and by the time he faced his biggest rival, he couldn't hold off Josh Warrington's inspired challenge. The hometowner was spurred on by 30,000 locals in Leeds and although Selby was beaten on points, he could at least ditch the unhealthy habits and move to a safer weight. It was a telling sign when he skipped super-featherweight altogether and made the overdue decision to go another division higher to lightweight.

"The last week [before fighting at featherweight], I'd probably have about a day's worth of calories all week. Hardly any nutritious food, nothing, just to get me by. It got to a point where I would make two meals, I'd chew up the one meal and spit it out. I'd replace it with a plate of lettuce leaves, that's how bad it got," shared Selby, who secretly grew fatigued from abusing his body to its limit.

"I'd never complain, I'd never tell my trainer or manager. I'd keep a straight face and make the weight. To me, failing the weight would be like losing a fight, it was like a fight to me. That's the stupid mentality of a boxer, I suppose. I couldn't tell my trainer or manager I'm struggling. It's not in a fighter's nature, I don't think."

Memories of losing his featherweight belt in an upset to Warrington may have lingered still. Nonetheless, the recovery process had made progress. A high ranking with the IBF and the organisation's Inter-Continental title, from an earlier win against American Omar Douglas in February, was a solid foundation to start a new chapter. An attempt at Welsh boxing history neared.

Photo: Liam Hartery

EX-SELBY OPPONENT IS FREE TO FIGHT AFTER POSITIVE DRUG TEST
Wednesday 6 November 2019

Andrew Selby (13-1, 7KO) had experienced more than most in his boxing career but an illogical subplot following his first professional defeat must have left the Barry man scratching his head.

Seven months after Julio Cesar Martinez (14-1, 11KO) beat Selby in a WBC eliminator, the Mexican power-puncher tested positive for a Clenbuterol, a performance-enhancing drug [PED]. Clenbuterol reduces blood pressure to enable more oxygen to be carried in the blood. It also enhances muscle growth and increases weight loss. The latter is particularly important in a sport where participants have to make weight limits – the eight stone flyweight category in this case.

The steroid-like chemical was originally developed to treat asthma in horses but there was a more concerning agricultural use in Mexico, where farmers routinely exploited it to increase the size of their livestock. For that reason, Martinez escaped without any sanctions when trace elements of the banned substance were detected in a doping test conducted by the Voluntary Anti-Doping Association [VADA] on behalf of the WBC.

The highest profile case of Clenbuterol happened in 2017 when multiweight world champion Saul 'Canelo' Alvarez tested positive. Boxing's biggest superstar – at the time – served a six-month ban imposed by the Nevada State Athletic Commission. The leniency of the decision was criticised at the time and Canelo returned to Nevada for a multi-million-dollar rematch with then-world middleweight champion Gennady Golovkin months later.

Many critics weren't convinced the authorities seriously scrutinized and appropriately punished the 'contaminated meat' excuse. Eyebrows were raised further when the World Anti-Doping Agency [WADA] took the decision to amend Article 7.4 of their code. It allowed WADA-accredited laboratories to report Atypical Findings [ATFs] of Clenbuterol and it meant that the threshold of allowable Clenbuterol in an athlete's body had been increased. WADA issued a Stakeholder Notice with the news and it was criticised by many recipients. The obligation to avoid detection of trace amounts of Clenbuterol was theoretically nullified for Mexican athletes, who had a ready-made excuse for positive tests. WADA insisted the change to their rules was necessary.

The WBC, now headed by Mauricio Sulaiman, welcomed the decision with open arms. In a statement to endorse the change of rules, the WBC said: "The WBC has received an additional report from VADA in which two

Mexican fighters showed atypical findings of Clenbuterol, which are well below the new WADA standard and all fighters will receive proper nutrition education from the WBC Clean Boxing Program and Weight Management Program. WBC champion Rey Vargas and WBC challenger Julio Cesar Martinez are at no fault with regards to their VADA atypical finding.

"Effective on June 1, 2019, the World Anti-Doping Agency (WADA) established a new threshold in relation to the detection of Clenbuterol. WADA's new standard intends to ensure that results management entities address and resolve positive anti-doping tests emanating from the consumption of contaminated meat products in a fair manner for the athlete. That will prevent athletes from being penalized for an anti-doping rule violation as a result of consuming contaminated meat.

"WADA's List of Prohibited List includes Clenbuterol because it promotes muscle growth through anabolic properties. However, scientific studies have shown to WADA's satisfaction that athletes can test positive for low levels of Clenbuterol after consuming contaminated meat. That finding has led to WADA reviewing their recommended results management rules governing adverse findings for Clenbuterol."

Decisions of this nature could have serious implications for sport in general. They could, and arguably did, open loopholes for doping scientists to take advantage of by tailoring their illegal programs. It was a complex and sensitive situation, especially in an age when users of PEDS were often a step, or light-years, ahead of testers.

Martinez stopped Selby with a body shot in the fifth round when they met in central Mexico. Fighting at more than 2,600 feet above sea level and arriving just five days before the fight wasn't ideal preparation for Selby. That much is undeniable. However, the possibility of facing a chemically enhanced opponent – whether intentional or not – was a challenge no boxer should encounter. The risk to health and life was already high enough.

The snakes and ladders nature of the business of professional boxing meant Selby was sidelined whilst Martinez prepared to challenge for the vacant WBC title in December. It was especially difficult for Selby to accept when the other corner would contain Cristofer Rosales (29-4, 20KO), a Nicaraguan trying to become world champion for the second time since losing to Selby in 2017.

The fight with Rosales would be Martinez's second shot at the crown. In August, Martinez thought he'd won the WBC belt when he left England's champion Charlie Edwards in a heap on the canvas. However, video replays showed Martinez landing a rib-smashing body shot when Edwards was on all fours and the knockout was swiftly changed to a no decision. The Englishman wisely opted to vacate his belt in the aftermath and head north to bantamweight, avoiding a rematch.

Boxing is rarely wise, nor boring.

EDWARDS AND WOODRUFF WITH THIRD ROUND THRASHINGS AT YORK HALL
Saturday 16 November 2019

London's York Hall was once again a happy hunting ground for Welsh boxers. Tonypandy's Rhys Edwards (8-0, 3KO) and Newport's Craig Woodruff (9-5, 3KO) both made statements with thrashing third round knockouts.

19-year-old Edwards, trained by Gary Lockett, extended his reputation as one of the UK's hottest prospects by halting Latvia's helpless Vladislavs Davidaitis (4-12, 4KO). The fearsome featherweight earned his stoppage by relentlessly unloading on Davidaitis and blocking every exit route. As expected, Edwards was quicker to the punch and very proactive, constantly initiating attacks and trying to create openings.

The beginning of the end came when Davidaitis received a pinpoint double left hook in the third round. It was delivered to his head and body, the second shot forcing Davidaitis to the floor. When he rose, Edwards used the same combination to shift his wounded opponent from the centre of the ring to the ropes. A series of right hands rained in and Davidaitis cowered, unable to get away from the onslaught. The only escape for the visitor came when referee Lee Cook was forced to jump between them.

"In the first two rounds, I was a bit amateur paced, I'd say, too fast. I went back [to the corner] and Gary said to slow down, open up and stop him. That's exactly what I done," analysed Edwards. "I was probably just a bit too eager, trying to impress too much but then I relaxed, took my time and got him out of there.

"My shot selection and placement of shots… I know I haven't got my man strength yet. It's coming and when I do get it, people will see the difference."

Every so often, a boxer comes through the ranks with talent that gets attention amongst all onlookers. Edwards' name had been whispered incessantly throughout Welsh gyms over the last two years. However, it was slowly starting to seep through to the mainstream scene a year after his professional debut.

Managed by Mo Prior, the prospect was kept busy with eight fights in his first 50 weeks as a professional. The activity made Edwards the most active boxer in Wales and he was eager to squeeze in another outing before Christmas. The hardest job facing Edwards' handlers was to hold him back. In the grand scheme of things, beating entry-level opponents wasn't that impressive but the easy manner in which the Welshman had done it stood out.

Edwards concluded: "He only caught me with a jab. It was a decent shot, not too good though. I can't wait for the step up now. Obviously, I'm still only 19, so I'm a kid but I'm progressing so fast. They can't hold me back forever. I'm going to take my time, keep listening and keep winning.

"I'll be back in December, maybe a six or eight rounder, just to tick over. Back out in the New Year, looking for titles. It's been an incredible year, especially seeing how much I've improved and come on. I can't wait to see what next year will bring, to be honest with you."

Later in the same ring, Woodruff made short work of London's Connor Marsden (3-1, 1KO). It was the contender's best performance for a number of years and he reminded everyone of his promise.

Marsden came with the confidence of an unbeaten prospect and Woodruff, who chose to appear in the away corner, was happy to bring him back down to earth. He spotted opportunities to catch Marsden by surprise and landed wide hooks when Marsden's chin was left exposed. The Englishman was as green as he was keen and Woodruff found the holes in his defence. After making a breakthrough and scoring two knockdowns, the third and final knockdown ended matters in devastating fashion. A right cross, left hook combination landed flush to send Marsden crashing down. He was unable to carry on and was stuck to the floor.

At six-foot, stepping up a weight category to super-lightweight was a relatively cosy transition for Woodruff. He still, however, planned to shed the pounds and return to lightweight, where he won the Welsh title in 2013. What followed that particular triumph over Tony Pace was a series of very tough opponents and questionable matchmaking, so it led to three straight losses. Woodruff, equipped with more experience, was determined not to make the same mistakes and he built a sturdy support structure around him. Since ending four years of inactivity from 2014-2018, 27-year-old Woodruff had linked up with manager Richie Garner and trainer Luke Pearce, nephew of Newport's heavyweight legend David Pearce. He recorded four wins from five fights and looked impressive on his return to boxing.

The show was promoted by Mick Hennessy and broadcast by terrestrial platform Channel 5. Both Edwards and Woodruff missed out on televised slots but strengthened their cases to be included next time. They also received strong support from a solid set of dedicated travelling fans, who made the cross-country journey from South Wales.

Photos: Liam Hartery & Spencer Love

WILLIAMS GOES FROM CLYDACH TO THE CONGO COPPER BOX
Monday 18 November 2019

Liam Williams (21-2-1, 16KO) was ready to head to Congo in search of a significant fight but the Clydach native would instead cross the Severn Bridge and venture to London's Copper Box Arena to end a frustrating few months of inactivity.

After destroying Joe Mullender in a British title defence in March, the middleweight captured the WBC Silver title with another explosive second round knockout of France's durable Karim Achour in July. He expected to kick on towards the top, only to endure prolonged uncertainty about his next steps towards world level.

Confusion was heightened in October at the annual WBC convention in Cancun, Mexico. Purse bids were called for Williams to make a defence of his 'silver' title against American contender Roberto Garcia. The bout was also intended to double up as a final eliminator to challenge the WBC's full champion, Jermall Charlo. Purse bids are essentially a private one-shot auction and the promoter willing to pay the largest sum of money is granted the rights to stage a fight. Some organisations demand that promoters pay a deposit for their participation, other organisations don't. To add to the gamble, the bids are submitted in sealed envelopes and any promoter can enter the auction. In this case, that's exactly what happened – it was won by Don King!

Earlier in King's life, the brash American promoter overcame stints in prison for serious violent crime, before becoming a major player in boxing for more than 30 years. Countless lawsuits and serious controversies followed him into boxing but it didn't stop him working with the likes of Muhammad Ali, Mike Tyson and Julio Cesar Chavez for some of their most infamous fights. By 2020, King's presence had drastically faded and his influence was next to non-existent.

Plans were promised for Williams and Garcia to fight in the Congo, central Africa. The only problem was that the official paperwork was missing and there was no hint of it showing up. Initially, Williams was ready for his own 'rumble in the jungle,' until his patience ran out after weeks of delays by King.

"It's one of those things… Don King is full of shit," vented Williams. "I was always in doubt that the fight was going to happen, let alone in Congo. Don King, I've had it up to my eyeballs with him.

"I don't even know the man, never set eyes on him but I think he's an absolute fucking prick. Just messing me around with this, that and the other. That's done with now and he's lost control of the situation."

The WBC eventually revoked King's right to stage the fight and Williams' handlers, MTK Global in management and Frank Warren's Queensberry in promotion, began to make their own plans. The training with Dom Ingle in Sheffield would finally be put to use on 21 December. London's Copper Box Arena, a site purposely built for the 2012 Olympics, was the location and BT Sport would be the broadcaster.

The date for Williams' return fell on the first anniversary of his faultless 10th round thumping of Manchester's unbeaten Mark Heffron and the British champion was hungry to repeat that feeling. The 27-year-old's feelings were usually expressed in a ruthlessly forthright fashion; he's a 'straight shooter' in and out of the ring. Coupled with a nasty finishing instinct in the ring, Williams' sound logic was sometimes overlooked or misunderstood.

"It's obviously been a long time waiting. I've been pulling my hair out for a little while now, just waiting and waiting, training my balls off every day," he sighed in a more relaxed tone than before. "I know something is coming, I know I'm going to fight before the end of the year. All the training I'm doing, I knew it wasn't going to go to waste but it's like… it's not the same training without a date.

"It's difficult because people know I'm getting a fight. I've got a decent following and people are texting me, asking what's going on. All these different questions and I've got to go along and just say that I'm waiting. I just want to fight!"

Williams had impressively recouped from contentious consecutive losses to Liam Smith in 2017. Nowadays, he was recognised by most people as the best current boxer in Wales and his status was reflected in his ranking with the WBC, who placed him at fifth in their hierarchy. Despite the delays, the ominously nicknamed 'Machine' was in position for a shot at any of the sport's top names. Williams didn't discriminate when names and belts were mentioned to him and he remained open to the WBO route, too.

He said: "I believe I should've been there [top five] before now if I'm honest. It's one of them things, you've got to take it as it comes. I'm happy with the position I'm in. I've got good rankings with the WBC and WBO. The next one could be a WBO final eliminator, or so I'm told. It's just one of them, I'm grateful for where I'm at, I'm in a good position with both governing bodies.

"In terms of opponents, I couldn't care less."

Photo: Huw Fairclough

GETHING GOES OUT OF GOLDEN CONTRACT TOURNAMENT
Friday 22 November 2019

Pontypool's Kieran Gething (9-2-2, 2KO) fiddled through a frustrating fight with London's Jeff Ofori (10-1-1, 3KO) and the official decision was a draw. However, 'Kiwi couldn't' find his way through the quarter-finals of MTK Global's Golden Contract tournament at super-lightweight.

96-95-94-96 and 95-95 tallies split the three judges and a 'winner' still had to be decided for the purposes of the tournament. It came down to the opinion of referee Kieran McCann who, without the aid of a scorecard, favoured Ofori and picked him to head to the semi-finals instead of Gething.

"I was disappointed. I think people could see that straight after the fight," sighed Gething. "The actual decision, the draw, I can come to terms with because I can see how they would score [rounds] for him but going out of the tournament like this is disappointing.

"It feels like an old-style newspaper decision. On the fullness of the fight, I think I boxed better than him, I think that's evident from the tape. I'm not disputing that he scored some really cracking shots on me, fair play to him. If you're going to take a fight on the whole like that, and just give the nod one way of the other, you should do it on the merit of the best boxer.

"Referee McCann's decision… it's the second time he' reffed me and the second time he's gone against me. I thought his refereeing was quite one-sided, as well."

Bowing out at the first stage of the Sky Sports televised event was an anti-climax for Gething. The Welsh champion hoped to tangle with the likes of ex-European champion Mohamed Mimoune, Ohara Davies and Tyrone McKenna. The winner of the tournament would secure a 'Golden Contract' worth $500,000 over two years. Gething left London's York Hall without the life changing money but gained plenty of other plus points from the occasion.

He said: "I am literally living what every young boxer's dream is. I'm fighting on ESPN and Sky Sports in the home of boxing. It feels like I've made it, y'know, what I set out to do. Now I just need some more belts in the cupboard to cement that."

The fight began well for Gething, who used a natural size and reach advantage to work behind the jab and find his range. Ofori didn't commit to much early on, focusing more on quality and he landed clean counters amidst Gething's rallies. It led to even exchanges when they met in the middle of the ring, but both timed their attacks differently. Gething was often more consistent throughout the three-minute duration of rounds, and Ofori spent a lot of time circling before launching a raiding attack in the final 60 seconds.

25-year-old Gething tried to be more assertive in the fourth round, using straights to drive Ofori backwards. Eventually, Ofori had enough of it and attempted to resist, rolling under Gething's arms and landing his own hooks. Keen to tighten up the gaps in his defence, Gething slowed the pace and got back to his boxing in the middle rounds. His more disciplined work reduced Ofori's chances to counter and he sat down on his shots with more authority. That was until round six finished with a full-on firefight.

They fought on the inside in the seventh round and Gething's more blatant approach drew a warning from the referee. It was slightly harsh and a sign of things to come. The last three rounds saw Ofori continue to work in spurts and his smart tactics kept him competitive until the end. Honest as ever, Gething could see the pros and cons to both approaches when he recalled how the action unfolded.

"There were some cracking right hands I lined up for him. I used my jab and it was much superior to his," considered Gething. "He caught me when he jumped in but had I had a bit more in the tank, maybe I could've pushed on a bit more.

"His arms look longer than they should be because he's a short guy. The bloke was five foot six [inches tall] and I was the one being told off for using my head. I don't understand that at all. He [the referee] was saying about me pushing him down but not about Jeff leaning in and I thought it was poor refereeing.

"He still managed get those long shots off on me. I think it was through my own faults. I feel like I say that a bit too regularly, but my own faults gave him gains. He's not a terrible boxer at all, he's quite evasive. The top half of his body is moving all the time. Maybe if I'd been a bit shorter or attacked the body, it could've slowed him down. He came in with a nothing to lose attitude."

As Gething accepted, there could be little complaint about the decision to award a draw at the final bell. The only gripe came with the method of the referee's decision, which omitted Gething from the tournament without the justification of a scorecard. That was, however, the rule of the tournament that the eight boxers signed up to. The saving grace was that at least it would go down as a draw on Gething's official record, rather than a loss.

Ofori's performance earned credit, especially since he'd been in action as recently as seven days earlier. On that occasion, he travelled to Liverpool to outhustle unbeaten local favourite Gerard Carroll. Ofori, a former Southern Area lightweight champion, showed little sign of fatigue in this night's 10 rounder.

The Golden Contract semi-finals would happen in 2020 and the intention was for the four eliminated boxers to face each other on the undercard. There was the added element that Gething could be drafted into the main tournament if there was an injury to one of the semi-finalists – after all, Ofori's inclusion came as a last-minute call up when Lewis Benson was ruled out on medical grounds.

"I've got four of them now [10 round fights on his record]," reflected Gething in closing. "I'd liked to have picked up more titles by now, to be honest. I wanted the Celtic title. That's the target for next year. Pick up another title and at least I know my capabilities with the 10 round distance."

Photo: Liam Hartery

EVANS EVENTUALLY SUCCUMBS TO TENNYSON IN FIGHT OF THE YEAR CONTENDER
Saturday 23 November 2019

If Craig Evans (20-3-2, 3KO) had punch power as big as his heart, the Blackwood native would stand towards the top of the sport.

Every boxer is brave, it's part and parcel of prizefighting, but the 30-year-old went beyond the call of duty in a barnstorming British title eliminator against Belfast's James Tennyson (26-3, 22KO). Evans rose from the floor and valiantly resisted before succumbing to the Northern Irishman's prolonged pressure in the 11th round at Liverpool's M&S Bank Arena.

Despite the disparity in power, Evans showed no hesitation in unloading early on. The southpaw reddened Tennyson's face with quick combinations and he then received a far more significant response before the opening round was over. Evans had a history of putting himself on the outskirts of the ring, a position usually used to tempt opponents into his type of fight. However, this position was exactly where Tennyson wanted Evans and a left-hook sagged the Welshman to his knees.

Evans turned professional in 2010 and this was the first time he'd been put down. He returned to his feet, clearly shaken and featuring a damaged right eye that was quickly worsening. Cutsman Billy Reynolds worked all of his magic to keep the swelling under control. Tennyson came flying out in the second round, keen to compound the effect of the injuries. Evans was brave and really dug in to survive the scare. Sucking up so much punishment at this stage of the fight was concerning and not a scenario Evans would've envisaged.

"When I was hurt in the first round, I took a knee because I was *hurt*. It was the first time I'd been down as a pro. It weren't nice," remembered Evans. "I was thinking, 'fucking hell, it's only the first round and God, I'm down.' I recovered well and the fight went as it went.

"The best thing to do was to take a knee, recover and come again. He hit me, hurt me and the best thing was to take a knee and recover. You go down, it's not nice to go down, but it [going down] was the best thing at the time. I was glad I did it because I could've been out of there in the first round."

The steely resilience was rewarded in the third round. Tennyson continued to come forward and Evans adapted. The Welshman was retreating on his own terms and his footwork kept him out of trouble. Vitally, Evans' jab was finally introduced to put space between the pair. Tennyson was made to look basic when Evans countered off the ropes and he was right back in a fight he looked destined to be bombed out of moments ago.

The remarkable recovery was evident in the middle rounds. Evans used his portside stance to square up Tennyson, who was becoming static in an attempt to return to his earlier authority. Even though Evans' shots weren't visibly hurting Tennyson, he was landing plenty of them and then doing a clever job of half-clinching to force referee Steve Gray to reset the pair. None of Tennyson's previous 21 knockouts had gone past the sixth round and Evans' belief grew.

Now it was Tennyson's turn to adapt. He did so with body shots and they impacted Evans' movement. Evans continued his own accurate activity throughout this period, though it lacked the same force as Tennyson. An accidental clash of heads cracked Evans' nose in the eighth round and caused further bleeding. It fired Evans up and after a short break to compose himself, he responded well by launching brisk flurries. More of Tennyson's accidental fouls followed and they further curbed Evans' work.

Tennyson landed a low blow in the ninth round and he was all-forearms in the 10th round. The referee wasn't happy with the moves and it was an indicator of Tennyson's mounting sense of frustration. The hidden price that Evans paid for clawing his way back into the fight was his sinking levels of stamina. Understandably, Evans slowed down and his guard loosened, unavoidably affording Tennyson chances to get back on top.

The end came in the 11th round. Tennyson beat Evans to the punch and landed a short hook. Evans had the instinct to hold but not the strength. Tennyson persisted and landed series of shots to force the referee to call a final halt to the dramatic fight of the year contender. Evans still resisted, even after it had ended.

"In the 11th round, he hit me but I was fine. The ref jumped in, which was sad like. There's nothing I can do about it, though. I just couldn't believe they stopped the fight," he said in defiance. "I boxed smart from round three up to round 10. The ref did what he had to do in round 11, I was gutted. I was hurt more earlier [in round one than round 11]. It is what it is.

"I was a bit tired. I got caught with my hands down, I took a step back, put my hands up and the ref stepped in, which I don't think he should have.

Since coming back home, everyone has said about it.

"He [Tennyson] is a good fighter. He hits hard but apart from that... he just kept coming forward, a busy fighter. I had to let me hands go or I was going to get hit, wasn't I."

Evans earned plenty of plaudits for his performance. Unfortunately, the absorbing encounter was embarrassingly omitted from the televised segment of the Matchroom show. It was instead placed on a Sky Sports internet stream for viewers on YouTube and Facebook. The bizarre decision backfired when several televised fights featuring ticket-selling locals failed to catch fire or inspire any sort of atmosphere.

Evans, unfussed by the snub, said: "You don't think about entertaining in the ring, I just do my job. Either way, I'm not bothered how entertaining it is but everyone has said it was fight of the night, saying how gutted they were that it wasn't on Sky and all that.

"It doesn't bother me. It is what it is at the end of the day. We both done our job and sometimes you get shown [on TV], sometimes you don't. It was a good fight and if it was shown live on Sky, the viewers would've got their money's worth."

It had always been Evans' intention to fight at the 130lbs super-featherweight limit, rather than five pounds heavier at lightweight. The opportunities, including a world title eliminator in Russia in 2018, had always come at the heavier weight and Evans' previous wins kept him there. A third defeat looked like the catalyst for change and the timing of it was crucial for the future of his career.

"I know I can take a shot at lightweight but I'm going to try and come down a weight now to super-featherweight and take it from there like," said Evans.

"Gavin [Rees - trainer] has always told me since I've come to the gym, I should be fighting at super-featherweight. I've been finding it too easy, I made it easy this time and it's better if I do come down.

"He [Gavin] is someone you look up to, a former world champion. He's giving me advice to learn from what he's done and been through. It's been going alright with him.

"Hopefully I can fight for another world title eliminator, try and get back up there, get the big money fights."

Photo: Liam Hartery

JENKINS' TITLE DEFENCE CUT SHORT BY HEAD CLASHES
Saturday 30 November 2019

For the fourth time in six fights, Swansea's injury-prone Chris Jenkins (22-3-3, 8KO) literally had his night cut short.

The welterweight champion was in Birmingham to defend his British and Commonwealth titles against Manchester's Liam Taylor (21-1-1, 10KO) and he might have been four seconds away from losing his beloved belts. An accidental clash of heads opened a huge cut over Jenkins' left eye and referee Steve Gray, in consultation with the ringside doctor, deemed it too severe to carry on after two minutes and 56 seconds of the fourth round. It meant the fight was ruled a technical draw but had it gone until the bell, it would've gone to the scorecards and Jenkins would've likely lost.

"Basically, in two words, pissed off," mused Jenkins when asked about his mood in the aftermath. "It happens every time when a fight is starting to catch fire. It always seems to be a head clash. I've heard people say it's because I'm making weight wrong, this and that. I'm making weight the best I've ever made it. I'm hydrated and it's nothing to do with that. It's because the shape of my head.

"I've got very prominent eyebrows, like a Neanderthal basically. If they [opponents] are gonna come in with the head and not even attempt to punch, it's gonna cut me open. I didn't really notice it in the amateurs but since I've joined Gary [Lockett – trainer], the boys in the gym always make fun of it [the shape of his face]. The last four or five years, I've really noticed it! The banter in the gym is immense but I've got thick skin like that."

After a nip and tuck opening round that Taylor probably pinched, it all kicked off in a memorable second round that was glorified by Queensberry's promoter Frank Warren. The duo met head on, shooting purposeful jabs before their power punches. Taylor was more assertive and he uncorked overhand rights. Jenkins decided to roll underneath Taylor's replies and he avoided most of them until he was clipped on the back of the head. The attempts to duck and sway out of the way failed and it sent Jenkins a short distance down to the floor. There were still more than two minutes of the second round left to go and it carried on with the same level of violence.

"The first round, I was seeing what he was made of. It was a very close round. Being the champion, I thought I would've nicked it but I've never had no favours in this game, so I thought I'd lost it," recollected Jenkins. "Second round, I was bobbing and weaving way too low. My feet were way too far apart. I lent over and he hit me on the back of my head. The force of the punch pushed me down but the impact was no problem at all. Me being me, I went to my old style and said 'lets go.' I was whipping in body shots, uppercuts and all sorts of stuff."

Jenkins, unwilling to play it safe, waged war when he stood up. He was determined to even the score and hurled two-fisted volleys to Taylor's body. The challenger was enthused and took his cue to battle back, looking for another breakthrough. Now it was Jenkins' turn to take advantage of his opponent leaning over, so he sent crunching uppercuts through the gloved gaurd. The Welshman was upping the ante and showed no lasting effects of the knockdown. It looked like Jenkins had it under control and then the session kicked off again. Taylor came right back into it in the final 30 seconds of the second round, shortening his longer leavers to rally in the pocket. Everyone took a deep breath when the bell rang to end a 'round of the year' contender. It had been exhausting to watch, never mind take part in, but Jenkins may have been the only person around who was underwhelmed by the entertainment.

He said: "I've watched the round because BT Sport put it up [online] under the headline 'what a round' but he just tucked up. He'd just dropped me, obviously with an illegal blow [on the back of the head] and I expected him to be swinging but he wasn't. He let me throw shots at him instead!"

The third round was quieter and Jenkins boxed with more caution, using his hand speed to initiate exchanges. He slowed the pace down with single shots and lots of Taylor's more pondering punches landed on the gloves. Nonetheless, Taylor persevered and his height was effective in parts, that was until he was on the receiving end in the fourth round. Jenkins finally appeared to be getting on top of him as he switched focus to Taylor's bigger body and the concentrated shot selection found the gaps in defence.

"I went back to the corner and had a right ticking off from Gary. I am scared of him. The only people I'm scared of is obviously my wife and Gary. I'm proper scared of him. He told me to jab and box his head off. The third round, that was what I was doing, keeping it simple and stuff," said Jenkins with a solid certainty.

"I was quite shocked at how long he was but I knew he was a good fighter. I've said before the fight, when it was announced, and I'll say it now, he deserved his spot."

The head clash happened at the end of the fourth round. Taylor's stance squeezed up and he slightly squatted over his front foot. Then Taylor crouched over more crudely and the crown of his head drove into Jenkins' face. Jenkins was no stranger to the warm sensation of claret leaking from his paper-thin facial skin. It was immediately called as an accidental head clash and led to the official result of a technical draw when the doctor provided his advice to the referee.

Speaking with more than a hint of suspicion, Jenkins had his own opinion on the final moments of the fight: "The fourth round, I caught him with little check hooks around the sides, I was getting into my groove. People are saying I'd have lost if the head clash went over to the next round. Listen, I'm not a four-round fighter, I'm a 12 round fighter. I honestly think down the line, I'd have stopped him late.

"I knew I was having a good round and his corner goes, 'get there now!' I threw a jab and all I felt was impact. It was like someone threw a brick at my head. I swore and all I could see was blood trickling through my eye. After the fight, I went into his changing room and they explained what they meant. They meant to get in, close the gap and work inside but… I've seen the footage and only they will know if that was the intention, if y'know what I mean. There was no feint to come in, no punch, none of that."

There was another equally disappointing side note. For the second time in seven days, a Welshman in an evenly matched British level fight was given the low priority 6:00pm slot on the running order. The fight opened BT Sport's broadcast and it was deserving of a far more prominent place on the televised segment of the show. Different network, very similar treatment.

Jenkins had long been lauded as the unluckiest man in Welsh boxing. A series of cuts and other unfortunate incidents, like fainting in front of BBBoC officials at a check weigh-in, had jinxed him for years. The turnaround in fortunes came when he received a voluntary shot at London's British champion Johnny Garton in March. Jenkins fulfilled his career goal with a 5/1 upset at the Royal Albert Hall and he added the Commonwealth title by beating Paddy Gallagher, another hometowner, on the road in Belfast. Those two wins, after years in the wilderness where short notice fights were his only option, helped to ease the latest episode of bad luck.

"It wasn't the way I wanted the fight to end. I wanted to end the year on a bang. I probably had the best year of my career but there's a few things in camp that didn't help us," he rationalized, alluding to unseen injuries. "At the end of the day, I'm still the British and Commonwealth champion. I'm a bit annoyed at the way this has happened but it is what it is. Rest up, heal and move on."

Serious flesh wounds were Jenkins' area of expertise and they'd become an unavoidable occupational hazard. Stitches and scars almost tempted Jenkins to walk away from the sport before his British title win. Now, at 31-years-old, Jenkins was being given the best possible chance to prolong his career and minimise the long-term lasting effects of the deep crimson cuts.

That was thanks to Dr Neil Scott, a BBBoC official and plastic surgeon, who went out of his way to help Jenkins' recovery.

"I've had 24 stitches from Dr Neil Scott. He's saved my career," said Jenkins. "He text me before the fight, 'If you get cut, I will sort you out tomorrow on my day off.' Surprise, surprise, I get cut and I get a text that night to call in on my way home. I was there on Sunday morning and he sorted me out."

The disappointment was easily rationalised and Jenkins refused to dwell on it. That mental fortitude was forged when he came through two personal tragedies that far outweigh the rollercoaster ride of boxing. The suicides of both of Jenkins' best friends, Darren Gates and Shaun Lewis, in August 2017 and April 2019, almost ended his enthusiasm for the sport. Suicide is the biggest killer of young men and wife Helen, who put her career as a carer on hold for her husband's boxing to take priority, was credited with helping him to come to terms with the tragedies. In response, Jenkins decided to use the memories of his friends as his motivation going forward.

"I'd lost my friend around the time I fought Darragh Foley [a technical draw due to cuts]. My best friend Gatesy took his own life and I was struggling outside of boxing. No-one knew about it," remembered Jenkins in a sobering tone, removed of the humour he usually exudes.

"Then, I got back in the gym and Gary said 'keep going, come on!' and the Garton fight come off. Then I'm champion and not so long after, my other close friend, Shaun, took his own life. Gary was concerned I was going to be stupid and fall out of love with the game. It's given me more drive. Them boys are up there, looking down and they keep me going."

The subject of mental health had a history of being wrongly stigmatised in macho environments, especially in boxing – a place where its importance should actually be magnified. The highs of fight nights are often met with lonely comedowns and Jenkins was well aware of the sport's emotional trampoline. He broke the mould just by talking about the vulnerabilities fighters face and showed a maturity not usually associated with the high-energy prankster that appears on the surface.

"I've been really down at times. When you win a fight, there are so many people texting you, everyone is your friend. Lose a fight and no-one wants to know you," he said, clearly speaking from experience. "They are hard times, they are. I've got the support of my wife, she keeps me mentally focused and I've got three kids to keep my mind busy. It's a number of things that all combine together and looking at where I am now, it's a dream come true.

"The next thing now is to win the British title outright [by winning three defences]. I'm a British level fighter, I'll take that all the way through but if I get a chance to box for something bigger, I'd be a fool not to go for it."

Photo: Huw Fairclough

CLASSY CORDINA MAKES MINI-STATEMENT IN MONTE CARLO
Saturday 30 November 2019

Most boxers often wait for a loss before making major changes but Cardiff's Joe Cordina (11-0, 7KO) decided to switch weight categories after a win.

The 28-year-old defended his British and Commonwealth belts against Welsh champion Gavin Gwynne at the O2 Arena in August. Two Welshman hadn't fought each other for the British title since 1994 and Cordina came through with a unanimous decision win after 12 physical rounds. It was tougher than many expected, partially due to Gwynne's sheer size and it contributed to Cordina's decision to shed five pounds and head south from lightweight to the 130lbs super-featherweight limit. The obvious benefit was that Cordina would now be the one to own a size advantage against opposition closer to his dimensions.

Mexico's Mario Enrique Tinoco (18-6-4, 13KO) was selected as the opponent and provided the perfect test to re-welcome Cordina to the weight class. They met on Matchroom's show in Monte Carlo, Monaco and Cordina produced a performance to match the stylish surroundings. Cordina came through with another unanimous decision win and the three judges rewarded his crisp shot selection with 98-92, 98-92 and 96-94 scorecards.

"I thought I was doing it [the weight] correctly until Dan Lawrence came onboard with my S&C [strength and conditioning]. He was helping me out with my nutrition and he totally changed the game for me," said Cordina, who had been under the lightweight limit days before he fought Gwynne.

"The people at world level at lightweight are bigger than Gavin [Gwynne]. Maybe not as tall but they're wide, thicker set and punchers. I'm not a big lightweight, I'm a big super-feather. It made sense for me to take it a bit more serious, be a bit more strict and change a couple of things. I made super-feather no problem. I was a pound under [the limit]."

Tony Sims, the Essex-based coach who took the reigns when Cordina left the 2016 Olympics, was full of praise. The softly spoken born-again Christian smiled in his analysis to Sky Sport's Andy Scott at ringside: "I thought he boxed really smart. He worked to orders and, as he was saying, the Mexican was a big puncher. You could see he was heavy handed on the inside.

"I thought his [Cordina's] long range shots were excellent, his hand speed was good and towards the end of the fight, he was mixing it up inside. Joe can work really good inside as well. Overall it was a good performance and a good learning fight. Don't forget, it was only his 11th fight."

Cordina quickly found his range in the first round. He fired accurate right crosses and oozed a calming confidence in front of the cameras. Tinoco edged forward, only to be met with a mixture of clever footwork and counters thrown from centre ring. In stereotypically Mexican fashion, Tinoco got busy with body shots to both sides in the second round. However, Tinoco also switched to southpaw and that wasn't a stereotypical trait.

Cordina said: "Tinoco looks a small man but he's boxed up at lightweight, super-featherweight and featherweight. He can go up and down and I've seen him at lightweight pushing people back. When he boxed Devin Haney [current WBC world lightweight champion], he had him on the back foot.

"I remember going to the press conference and David Diamante [Master of Ceremonies] said, 'Joe, don't take this geezer lightly. He's the real deal, he's just under top level and he can cause a lot of people problems. Be careful.' I don't take anyone lightly."

Cordina had to adapt to thwart the dynamic threat and Tinoco got his wish in the third round as Cordina met him head. The 'Welsh Wizard' blocked and countered straight down the pipe, before pivoting to the sides and resetting the exchanges to go again. It kept Tinoco unsteady and he even walked back to the wrong corner at the end of the round until his cornermen ushered him to his stool for a minute of rest.

Referee Jean Robert was hardly needed as the pair sorted themselves out, barely holding or spoiling the action for a breather. Tinoco was always looking to get stuck in and that eagerness worked against him. Cordina's movement opened the angles for piercing uppercuts, before he decided to stamp his authority in the fifth round. The meatier shots were usually long right hands or wide hooks to the body, around the sides of Tinoco's high guard.

"Tony wanted me to keep pivoting but I was so much physically stronger than him," said Cordina of his more direct approach. "I felt like on the inside, he ain't gonna do anything I've not done in sparring. I was sparring welterweights! I was practicing staying on the inside and pivoting around, making them miss and catching them straight away, not even with a hard shot. I felt really, really confident."

Tinoco started the second half of the fight with a renewed energy. The well-known Mexican body shots landed and it was reassuring when Cordina remained calm, confident in his ability to handle the hassle. Cordina then enjoyed a strong finish to the sixth session, gracefully shooting straights like he was aiming a bow and arrow. There was no sign of the unbeaten operator being worn down and he started to diversify his attack in the seventh. The most impressive eye-catcher came when Cordina unrolled two soft uppercuts upstairs, only intended to divert Tinoco's attention away from the third punch, which was a stinging left hook to the body. It was a show of regal skills and won favour with new fans in the crowd, including Prince Albert II of Monaco.

The last two rounds saw Cordina continue to pull away. The former amateur star was well-known for his silky skills at long range, so the revealing of his ability up-close was a welcome sight. It called on all of Tinoco's guts and his attempts to override Cordina never slowed. That ambition won Cordina's respect, leading to a sporting embrace at the end of the 10 rounder.

Studying the flow of the fight, Cordina said: "You know he's got that physical strength. When I boxed him, in the second round I thought, 'okay, I've got to be wary here.' When I got on the inside in round four and I started working, I felt the life drain out of him. By rounds seven and eight, I started putting shots together and it felt quite easy in there. The size of me at super-featherweight will play a part in my fights.

"I knew I had to be on my a-game. To be honest, it felt like when I was in there, I could've done another five rounds. It felt like I didn't have to step up any gears. I only had to stay in one gear and just be smart, don't take any big risks. I felt so much physically stronger than him. I knew this guy couldn't cause me any problems at all."

It was no surprise to see Tinoco last until the final bell. The 29-year-old hard man had recently upset Nottingham's much-fancied prospect Jordan Gill and lasted the distance with current WBC champion Devin Haney. Cordina handled him as well as anyone else and all the indicators were pointing to higher levels. The WBA Continental bauble didn't mean a lot in the bigger picture. However, its involvement signalled Eddie Hearn's intentions for Cordina to climb the world rankings and target the titles at the top.

"I think I'm number 18 on BoxRec in the super-featherweight division. I'm slowly getting there. [Carl] Frampton and Jono Carrol are the only ones in the British and Irish isles that are above me. I'm ninth with the WBA and I'm in the IBF rankings also. Slowly but surely, I'm getting there. Three fights or maybe four and I'll be ready for a world title.

"I'd fight anyone for a world title. If they said [it was possible] tomorrow, I'd jump at it. For me, I'd tell them I've been in camp constantly. I'm lying but I'd take my chances! Any of the world champions, I'd take them.

"If I had my way, I would go straight to the world title and that's what I'm aiming for."

Photo: Huw Fairclough

GWYNNE'S QUICK KO SETS UP ANOTHER SHOT AT THE BRITISH TITLE

Saturday 30 November 2019

Trelewis' Gavin Gwynne (12-1, 2KO) began the ascent towards a second shot at the British title in striking fashion.

The Welsh lightweight champion kept his tools sharp by quickly disposing of Cameroon's Abdon Cesar (4-11) in a first round knockout. The two-minute appearance headlined Sanigar Events' show in Pontypool and it was a very different setting to his last fight. Three months earlier, the 29-year-old was grinded out by Cardiff's Joe Cordina in a challenge for the British and Commonwealth titles. It took place under the bright lights of a Sky Sports Box Office undercard in London.

"No matter where you're fighting, it's still a ring. Fighting at the O2 [Arena] or fighting in Pontypool, you're fighting at the end of the day," said Gwynne, who was practical about the transient switch of scenery. "You've got to get up for it, you've got to get it in your head that there's someone in the other corner coming to take your head off."

Gwynne was working to finish the scheduled eight rounder inside the distance as soon as the bell sounded. He towered over Cesar and two right crosses in the opening 30 seconds sent the recipient onto his heels. Those shots were enough to convince Cesar to back off and Gwynne shadowed in quick pursuit. For a tall boxer, Gwynne was deceptively effective up close and it took Cesar by surprise. The 29-year-old wasn't known for his power but his sheer size caused problems for anyone at this level. Cesar momentarily stuck to the ropes and Gwynne landed his favourite shot, a left hook to the liver. A second left hook, this time thumping the head, moved Cesar off the ropes and he was clearly unsettled by Gwynne's constant inspection.

The end came as Gwynne unleashed a thumping overhand right. It detonated high on the side of Cesar's head, almost behind his ear, and it crumbled him to the canvas. Referee Chris Jones took up the count and Cesar met the mandatory eight count, only for his body language to suggest he had little interest in continuing for another seven rounds.

"I hit him with a hook to the body and to the head. He gasped for air and then I hit him with an uppercut, another left hook and he went sprawling to the other side of the ring," said Gwynne, reliving his first knockout in three years. "I thought 'I've got him, I've only got to catch him clean.' That's what I done. It was a temple shot and he just went down.

"I thought I'd go to the body because he did have a hard head and he hurt my hand. The right hook I threw, the one he dropped to, really hurt my hand. I was glad he didn't wanna carry on after it.

"One of the things I've been working on in the gym is trying to get my shots off from range. I've got more leverage in it. A fighter I really look up to is [WBA world super-middleweight champion] Callum Smith. The type of style he fights [with] is exactly like mine. He can fight inside but he boxes really well on the outside and puts his shots together, that's what I'm going to try and do."

Cesar represented Cameroon at the 2012 Olympics in London and was part of the squad to defect and stay in England. The 34-year-old, based in County Durham, had fought on the road as a professional and found it tough. Cesar had mainly fulfilled his role as an away fighter but there was a handful of occasions when he upset home favourites. In October, he travelled to Liverpool to turn over local favourite Steve Brogan and that upset was fresh in Gwynne's mind.

"Going off his last performance, he beat Steve Brogan. I watched a couple of clips on YouTube and I thought I was in for a hard night," chuckled Gwynne in reflection. "He looked tough but I seen a couple of chinks in his armour. Every time he got caught clean with a body shot, he'd like freeze but Brogan didn't switch on to it.

"I can punch but obviously, at the start of my career, I was held back and told not to stop these guys because it's harder to get matched up as you're going through the ranks. Before this fight, they said to me 'don't go hanging about in there, if you can get this geezer out of there, get him out of there.' That was in my head straight away, as soon as I come out. I wanted an early night."

It was Gwynne's first fight since the captivating challenge to Cordina in August. Gwynne exceeded the pre-fight expectations of everyone except himself and appeared to influence Cordina's return to super-featherweight. Initially reluctant to accept praise for a losing effort, Gwynne's stance has softened and the passing of time has helped him to look back at the experience in a different light.

He said: "I was gutted for the first couple of weeks after I lost to Joe but I had a lot of positives to take from it as well. I didn't disgrace myself. It was a close fight. I've watched it back a couple of times and to be honest with you, it was only a couple of rounds in it. He had a good start but other than that, it's been a fantastic year and hopefully I'll have an even better 2020."

It was understood that Cordina would vacate the titles after his triumph against Mario Enrique Tinoco in Monaco. Gwynne was hungry for the silverware and well positioned in the BBBoC pecking order. The chance was likely to come against Belfast banger James Tennyson, who conquered Blackwood's Craig Evans a week earlier. The explosive Northern Irishman presented a formidable task.

"It'd be fireworks from the off. I wouldn't take a backwards step and let him bully me," assured Gwynne. "Hopefully in the new year, we get a call. James Tennyson obviously won an eliminator against Craig Evans, what a fight that was. I'm going to stay in the gym over Christmas and stay ready, just in case I get that phone call.

"I'd say he's world class, if I'm honest. The only guys he's lost to are very skilled operators like Tevin Farmer [IBF world champion]. He's a fantastic fighter but I think at super-featherweight he [Tennyson] was killing himself to make the weight. At lightweight, he's a lot better and I think he's a lot stronger.

"Of course I'd travel. I'd fight anyone and I'd fight them anywhere. Obviously when I boxed Joe, I had to go all the way up to London. As two Welsh boys, it would've been nice to have it in Cardiff but I'll fight anywhere for the British title. I really don't mind.

'At the end of the day, it's still a boxing ring. It doesn't matter where it is."

Photo: Liam Hartery

SANIGAR EVENTS SHOWCASE SMALL HALL TALENT IN GWENT
Saturday 30 November 2019

Sanigar Events ventured to Pontypool to hold the last professional boxing show on Welsh soil in 2019. The eight-fight event at the Active Living Centre showcased several up and coming talents from Gwent and the wider South Wales area.

It took a prolonged four hours to get through 30 rounds of fights. The delays were due to the late arrivals of two of the away corner boxers but locals were rewarded for their patience with a small hall classic in the chief supporting slot.

Risca's Jake Tinklin (5-0) took a risk in stepping up to fight the experienced Zoltan Szabo (27-23, 12KO) and he took even more risks in the way he went about earning a narrow 58-57 decision win.

The 22-year-old was ordered by trainer Gavin Rees to use his skills and box but Tinklin just couldn't resist a tear up. The pair squared up at short range and took turns to unload heavy hooks. Tinklin owned the greater height and reach, only to surrender them in the first round and meet Szabo in centre ring. There was more sense on show in the second round as Tinklin slashed clean straights from long range. Szabo tried to duck under Tinklin and did so with some success. He was met with a jab in the third round and responded by rushing Tinklin to take advantage of the Welshman's stationary feet.

A sense of concern grew amongst the crowd in the fourth round. Tinklin was backed up to the ropes, stood too tall with his head high and he decided to trade with Szabo. It led to uncomfortable exchanges, with neither paying a lot of attention to defence. Tinklin matched Szabo punch for punch but he left the round with a bloody nose, having ignored calls from the corner for discipline. The fifth and sixth rounds saw Tinklin return to his jab to the relief of the partisan audience. Tinklin passed the gut check long ago, now he was belatedly passing a test of tactical savviness. To Szabo's credit, his effort never relented and the Hungarian played his part in a small hall fight to remember.

Cardiff's Lloyd Germain (3-0) opened the show by beating a southpaw for the first time as a professional. The busy welterweight earned a 40-36 scorecard by outworking MJ Hall (2-47-2), who was happy to tuck up and last until the final bell. 29-year-old Germain faced little resistance but it was still the most polished performance he'd produced, calculating short right hands with increasing effect over the 12-minute duration.

Port Talbot's Geraint Goodridge (4-10-3) enjoyed a rare appearance in the home corner and savored it by beating Jordan Grannum (5-67-2) over six rounds. The middleweight threw a lot more than his visitor, occupying attention with short bursts of hooks in the early exchanges. Goodridge ploughed on in the middle rounds and Grannum tried to respond, but without the prevalence to cause any trouble. The bigger will to win belonged to Goodridge, a former Welsh league footballer, and it proved to be the difference on the official 59-56 margin. It was the first time Goodridge had recorded consecutive wins since 2017.

Ystrad Rhondda's youngster Jordan Withers (2-0) was a class above scrappy survivor Victor Edgaha (2-70-3) but he couldn't get the Italian out of there. Formerly a Welsh international amateur, Withers kept Edgaha disturbed and settled for a 40-35 points win. The middleweight changed the heights of his attacks and Edgaha swung wildly in an attempt to ease the pressure. Withers landed with crisp power punches in the closing stages and Edgaha did well to avoid more damaging blows, until he was blasted by a right cross in the fourth round. It scrambled Edgaha's senses and he awkwardly fell over. Edgaha improvised to avoid being finished, which included conveniently losing his gum shield.

Port Talbot's pivoting Joshua John (2-0) ducked and darted his way around Ricky Leach (3-49-1), excelling in a flashy 40-36 decision win. There were times when Leach attempted to force the action but most of his moves backfired as John negated the natural size difference. John, a natural bantamweight and GB amateur champion, was up at featherweight and keen to keep his distance. The 25-year-old used all sorts of angles to throw quick combos and Leach was never able to catch up.

Bridgend's Robbie Vernon (5-0, 3KO) was too hot for Michael Mooney (9-72-2, 3KO) to handle and he smashed his way to a knockout win in less than 60 seconds. The 24-year-old super-lightweight prospect wasted no time in introducing himself to Mooney. Vernon troubled the Midlander with a series of relentless hooks as soon as he found his range. Mooney found himself trapped in the corner and could barely move an inch as southpaw bombs were pitched in. The energetic attack forced referee Chris Jones to end the action early. The switch-hitting Welshman continued to make a serious impression on the small hall scene, suggesting his future would be fun.

Photo: Liam Hartery

OLYMPIAN EVANS REKINDLES HIS HUNGER AND UNBEATEN THOMAS TICKS ON
Saturday 7 December 2019

As Anthony Joshua reclaimed his world heavyweight crowns against Andy Ruiz in a Saudi Arabian desert, another finalist from the 2012 Olympics also aimed to recover from his first knockout loss as a professional, though in very different surroundings and circumstances. Cardiff's Fred Evans (6-1) was 4,000 miles away in Southampton. There were no major honours or multimillion-pound purses at stake as Evans took the first steps of an important rebuilding job.

The talented 28-year-old had stuttered since claiming a silver medal at the Olympics and he'd gone in a very different direction to Joshua. After a few brushes with the law postponed the start of Evans' professional career, he got underway and recorded five wins. It was going smoothly, at least from the outside looking in, until it was brought to a shuddering halt 14 months ago. In less than five minutes, Evans unravelled at the unexpected hands of Ryan Toms, a handy operator with an even win-to-loss ratio, and it was a painful blow to his lofty expectations. Half-hearted training sessions and too much time in the sauna had caught up with Evans in two shattering rounds. It was a real wakeup call and Evans then decided to part ways with management Sanigar Events and trainer Tony Borg.

In a complete shakeup, Evans headed to Gary Lockett in Llanrumney, Cardiff and the appearance on the south coast was their first outing together. The southpaw stalked Bolton's Chris Jenkinson (11-72-3, 4KO) in a four round rust-shredder and he came away with a whitewash 40-36 decision win, tallied by veteran referee Jeff Hinds.

"That was the best I've felt since my six others [fights]. It was definitely the best I've felt," reckoned Evans as he cooled down and carefully took his hand wraps off in the changing room. "After the first round, I felt good in myself, sharp and I was able to step on the gas a bit.

"Obviously, he was well-experienced, he was keeping out of the way and he was hard to track down. Everything just went to plan though. I feel a lot sharper, stronger, fitter. I know I'm going in there now, 100% fit. I've got the confidence, I'm going in there as a happy fighter.

"It [training] has been excellent. I've been sparring with Maredudd [Thomas], Chris Jenkins, Nathan Thorley. I've done a lot of sparring. I think in March, we've got another show in Cardiff. I'll be on that, hopefully for a six rounder or more and I'll just keep on it now, obviously step it up a gear. I definitely want to look for some titles, whatever Gary and the management team think."

Evans, with his low right lead, gradually reduced the distance over the 12-minute duration. The approach allowed Evans to flick a jab from his waist, distracting Jenkinson from the more hurtful punches. Left hooks landed when Jenkinson tried to turn away from the ropes and Evans was judging his range with all the style expected of an ex-amateur star. As viewers often witnessed in the unpaid code, Evans stayed perfectly well balanced and his class was evident as he picked holes in Jenkinson's guard. Jenkinson was well aware of the difference in levels and he rarely threatened to throw if Evans was within punching distance. Understandably, Jenkinson maintained a compact defence and Evans focused on the body, where the target was bigger.

The attacks came with more meaning in the third round and Evans increased his attention to Jenkinson's inflamed frame. It became messy in the fourth round and the referee lamented both for their attempts to wrestle away from clinches. Still, it didn't distract from the purpose of the fight and Evans, relieved at being back in a ring, smiled at the final bell. The first comeback fight was out of the way. As expected, Evans had a win under his belt and he was back on the horse. Job done.

Promoter Steve Bendall, a former English champion, was thankful for two Welsh additions. Evans was joined on the show by Cardiff's welterweight Maredudd Thomas (10-0, 2KO) and the duo boosted a line-up that featured just five fights at Southampton's Central Hall. 23-year-old Thomas got the night's action underway against the winless Carl Turney (0-11) and the late notice fight saw the Welshman extend his unbeaten record. Referee Jeff Hinds scored the four rounder 40-35 to Thomas, who dominated it from start to finish.

Thomas marched forward and discouraged any hope Turney dared to consider during a subtle stare off prior to the first bell. 'Merv', as nicknamed by his gym mates, then looked to land uppercuts when Turney tucked up.

Body shots turned Turney's body to an angry shade of pink by the end of the first round but the journeyman did manage to land a right hand in the closing stages. It was a reminder for Thomas to stay switched on.

Turney, stimulated by the earlier moment, showed more ambition at the start of the second round. Thomas blocked the traffic coming his way and his accurate replies found room to land through Turney's wider hooks. The third round saw Thomas commit with his own hooks. A sustained onslaught cornered Turney and he was dropped to the floor. The follow up attack called on all of Turney's willpower. He continued but there was little chance for rest, even when the bell rang as Turney was forced to eat a flush uppercut in the last second of the round.

Blood began to run from Turney's nose in the fourth round and Thomas upped the pressure again. Turney had a knack of stopping the action by holding at just the right times and those survival skills even featured a clumsy rugby tackle to trip both boxers to the floor. Thomas landed a hurtful right cross a millisecond before the illegal move and it explained Turney's decision to try the tackle, which earned a justified warning from the referee.

"[He was a] tough boy, I caught him with a good few shots," stated Thomas, as he packed his bag and got ready to head 130 miles to home. "In the last round, I caught him and he dragged me down with him. [The fall] bust my knuckle up a little bit. That should've counted as a knockdown as well, I thought. I'm happy with the performance, though.

"I knew I had him hurt but he punched hard himself, to be fair to him. He could bang a bit, I felt I took his shots fine, he didn't trouble me. To be honest, I prefer that [being punched at] than having opponents run away because you're chasing them and it looks bad then, doesn't it? With him, he kept me on my toes and I was trying to catch him when he was coming in, so it gave me opportunities."

The win sealed what Thomas' hoped to be the end of his apprenticeship. He was keen to move to higher levels and more competitive matchups. The fight was especially pleasing as Thomas was originally scheduled to fight on Mo Prior's show at the Vale Sports Arena in November. However, the show was cancelled with less than a week to go.

"As soon as I can, 100%," Thomas answered purposely when asked about his future plans. "We're pushing for March next year. Hopefully I'll have a good step up fight against someone unbeaten or with a solid record. I think that's when I'll perform my best; when someone is coming forward and I catch them with shots. As soon as he started throwing shots at me tonight, that's when I caught him and put him down.

"Whenever Gary or Mo [Prior – manager] want me to fight for a Welsh title, or any other title that comes up, I'm happy to fight for it."

Evans and Thomas, who both entered fatherhood in recent months, pushed Gary Lockett's run as a coach to a 40-fight unbeaten streak. The achievement continued to build momentum for the most active professional gym in Wales.

Photos: Huw Fairclough

CALZAGHE'S CAREER CELEBRATED WITH LIFETIME ACHIEVEMENT AWARD
Tuesday 10 December 2019

It had been 11 years since Joe Calzaghe (46-0, 32KO) called time on his legendary career, but the unbeaten Welsh boxer's achievements were still celebrated like they happened yesterday.

The Newbridge native travelled across Gwent to the Celtic Manor Resort in Newport for the BBC Wales Sports Personality of the Year awards. Calzaghe, now 47, received the lifetime achievement award.

The award was reserved for individuals who had dedicated a lifetime to sport in Wales and it was presented by Baroness Tanni Grey-Thompson, the pioneering Paralympic champion and last year's winner. However, Calzaghe was quick to divert praise to his late father and sole trainer, Enzo, who passed away in 2018 at just 69-years-old.

"It's a long road, 27 years of boxing. From the first moment, as an eight-year-old, my father brought me to Newbridge's boxing gym and trained me," he began his acceptance speech alongside host Gethin Jones. "He always believed in me. A lot of people didn't believe in me… it wasn't always natural. I had injury problems; I had a few losses as an amateur.

"This is not just for me, to be honest. It's also for my father because if it wasn't for him, always believing in me when people didn't believe in me and giving me the confidence and dedicating his life to me," he paused as the crowd broke into spontaneous applause. "… nothing would be possible. Thank you, Dad."

Enzo's impact, which began with basically no background in boxing, was unprecedented. It led to Gavin Rees and Enzo Maccarinelli's world title triumphs, also influencing the careers of Nathan Cleverly, who went on to do the same, and Kerry Hope, who later won the European title. All of Enzo's relentless energy for boxing was spent in the most modest of settings; first in a little blue shed above a stream and then in an old rugby clubhouse. Both locations were unlikely launchpads but Enzo used both to guide Welsh boxing to the top of the world.

Joe's achievements were well known; 20 world title defences at super-middleweight and every world title belt collected, before he cemented his status in America by becoming lineal light-heavyweight champion. It was a lengthy dominance that Welsh boxing was unlikely to see repeated anytime soon.

What was equally impressive was Calzaghe's reluctance to come back to boxing. The sport is littered with cautionary tales of boxers who were tempted by one more fight, only for it to flop and damage their reputation. Admiration of Calzaghe's career was no doubt enhanced by the evergreen contentment he enjoyed from his decision to retire at the top.

He said: "Everyone talked about going to 50-0 but legacy was the biggest thing for me. Being a champion and retiring from boxing, not boxing retiring me… Obviously, you always get the carrot of big money, big paydays and for years afterwards I still got called out but I'm happy to be able to be here in front of my family [and] my boys there. Like I said, it's an honour."

Later on, Ystrad Mynach's Lauren Price was beaten to the Wales Sports Personality of the Year award. Welsh rugby captain Alun-Wyn Jones received the award for his leadership during a record-breaking run of form that stretched to 14 consecutive wins, a Six Nations Championship and the semi-finals of the World Cup. Price's European and world honours as an amateur were special accomplishments, yet nothing was ever likely to outshine a successful rugby star in Wales.

Photos: Huw Fairclough

LOCKETT'S STABLE INCREASES UNBEATEN STREAK TO MEET MILESTONE
Saturday 14 December 2019

Gary Lockett's Llanrumney-based stable reached a major milestone by extending its unbeaten streak to 40 fights.

Tonypandy's Rhys Edwards (9-0, 4KO) and Cardiff's Nathan Thorley (14-0, 6KO) both collected wins on Mo Prior's show at London's York Hall. The duo's latest victories added to a remarkable record that the team started building in May 2018. A total of 11 boxers contributed to the record, including Jay Harris, Alex Hughes, Fred Evans, Chris Jenkins, Jacob Lovell, Shokran Parwani and Maredudd Thomas. The only slight hiccup in that 19-month spell came when Jenkins shared a frustrating technical draw with Liam Taylor a fortnight earlier.

"It's been a massive year for the gym. I'm very lucky to have the fighters I've got. Don't forget, a trainer is only as good as the fighters he has and I have a lot of talent there," calmed Lockett when questioned about the notable record. "Credit to them all, they all work very hard. Luckily enough, we've not had any defeats and we're looking forward to 2020. Hopefully we see Jay Harris in a big title fight and a couple of the boys fighting for British titles as well."

The latest outing in London was an early start. Thorley appeared at the top of a running order that featured 19 other fights. The cruiserweight entered the ring at 3:00pm and there were few observers present, other than the usual diehard loyalists and BBBoC officials. Thorley prevailed with a 40-37 decision win against Lithuania's Dmitrij Kalinovskij (13-62-4, 5KO). The former Welsh light-heavyweight champion didn't produce his best form in the four rounder, which saw him faced with an opponent tall enough to be a good-sized heavyweight. However, a second fight in three months gave Thorley a reason to smile. The 26-year-old hadn't been happy under previous management and his two outings at the end of 2019 at least kept him active ahead of a planned return to title fights in 2020.

"Nathan didn't perform very well at all," said Lockett, once again calming in his answer. "He got the 'W' and done enough to win but he didn't look himself. He did alright in the first round, the second round was harder and I changed the tactics then. We just have to say, a win is a win and we move on to improve for the next one.

"Everything happens for a reason. He's 14-0 and he needs a *'fight'* now. Simple as that. Sink or swim in the New Year. February or March time, we'll put him in with someone with a similar record to himself. Hopefully you'll see the best Nathan Thorley then."

Edwards featured further up the running order and he folded Bulgaria's Stefan Sashev (5-27-1, 5KO) in two swift rounds. The 19-year-old capped off his first year as a professional by gracing the iconic venue for a fifth time. Edwards earned rave reviews in the English capital and the dynamic left hook he detonated on Sashev's body made waves further afield through social media, where it bordered on becoming 'viral' content.

Lockett said: "I'm really happy with the progress. He's not fighting people at the moment where they're trying to win, so I think we ought to put things in perspective. However, it's the way that he's doing it, he's doing it without taking a punch and it's very impressive. I think he needs to grow up a little bit, mature and knuckle down a little bit more. Having said that, if he continues to operate in the way that he is, he's got a big future.

"If he keeps on progressing like he is, you can't hold him back. That has resulted in me taking a fight against Johnny Phillips (5-3, 2KO) on February 15th. If he beats Johnny Phillips, which we expect him to, we're not going to start running before we can walk. Johnny Phillips is up a level to the guys he's been fighting and we'll stay at that level for two or three fights and look to push him into an eight rounder after that."

As the most active boxer in Wales in 2019, Edwards garnered a lot of attention and it was more than novice professionals on the small hall scene usually receive. Lockett was keen to keep a lid on the praise and expectation for now, mindful that there's still a lot for his boxer to learn. It was a sensible and rare standpoint; those who are responsible for guiding young boxers are often quick to hype their interest as 'the next big thing.' To assist the learning, Lockett also oversaw the selection of opponents, all chosen to bring something different to the table to benefit Edwards' education.

"I've done it all myself a million times, I've made all the mistakes. I've gone through everything they're going through," explained Lockett, recalling the knowledge from his own 12-year professional career. "At times, Rhys is a good listener when it comes to boxing instructions. He was trying to box like I told him to do in the first round and he looked really good. I just said to him, 'if you stick to the boxing, the openings will come.' I know it's the oldest thing you can tell a fighter but he did that and it came.

"What's been important with Rhys, we've given him a variety of opponents where he's had someone who runs, someone who comes at him a bit, a southpaw, someone who backs off. It just gives him different options to learn against different styles of fighters. I think we've done that for nine fights and now we have Johnny Phillips. It's a different style again, Johnny has a winning record and he'll come to win. He'll give a little bit of mouth as well which is different for Rhys to handle."

It hadn't all been plain sailing for Lockett in recent years. When Liam Williams suffered back-to-back defeats to fierce rival Liam Smith in 2017, the respective controversial and contentious circumstances didn't lessen the pain. Shortly after in June 2018, Williams decided to part ways with Lockett and link up with Dominic Ingle in Sheffield. Lockett received widespread praise for the way he handled the harmonious split, wishing Williams well in his move to freshen things up. The refreshing 'boxer first' attitude was possibly influenced by his own experiences in changing trainers when he was a boxer.

"These things happen in boxing. People are always going to leave you; no matter how close you are to them or whatever happens. It's inevitable and I think it's very important not to take these things personally," said Lockett, without a trace of hesitation. "That doesn't mean it was easy for me, of course it wasn't and it still isn't. I've had success before Liam, I've had success since and I'd like to think I'll continue to have success, not only as a trainer but as a manager as well. I'm really enjoying it and it's really good to be in my position. I'm really lucky."

A temporary dip in Lockett's enthusiasm for boxing would've been natural. However, the opposite occurred and he more than retained his drive to work with the rest of the stable, which quickly featured fresh recruits. They were housed in Llanrumney Phoenix Amateur Boxing Club [ABC], a community-conscious facility in the heart of the east of Cardiff. Williams even popped in for tick over training sessions when he was back home in the Rhondda valleys. The newbies and regulars created a strong team bond and any signs that the gym lost its leading light were difficult to find. If anything, the latest chapter for Lockett's stable had actually resembled a renaissance.

Lockett projected an intimidating exterior during his own fighting days, which ended with a challenge to WBC and WBO world champion Kelly Pavlik in 2008. It was no secret that the big punching middleweight lost the love for boxing around that time, only to discover it again when passing on his knowledge as a trainer, manager and mentor in the years following. Nowadays, a cast of jokers benefitted from his guidance. Laughter eased the testing training regime and the coping mechanism was usually led by Lockett.

The 43-year-old's reputation as a practical and methodical teacher had seen his influence extend to MMA. Lockett was brought on board as a striking coach for Bellator contender Lew Long and rising UFC star Jack Shore. His role as a consultant fitted in alongside experts from other disciplines, such as jiu jitsu and wrestling, to reflect the complex nature of the combat sport. Boxing wasn't usually willing to learn from MMA, a relatively new phenomenon that had grown at a rapid rate over the course of 20 years. In the established etiquette of traditional boxing training, the voicing of numerous opinions was usually avoided. The reason for the old school of thought was that it usually ended in mixed messaging and eventual defeat. However, Lockett was confident he could apply a similar approach to his boxing.

"Basically, it's something I've grown to do now because I've got the people handy but back in the beginning, I never had the resources or people offering their help. Now, people offer their help and they're all a good part of the team. Don't get me wrong, if I wasn't confident they could do what I wanted them to, I wouldn't have them involved. These guys have been true to their word and been really good. There's good trust and that's very important.

"It's important to have lots of people around you, rather than trying to do everything yourself because you can't. I've got seven fighters to train, a few more to manage and two little terrors at home. I'm not a millionaire so I can't be in the gym 24/7 after work as well."

Whilst laid back, Lockett recognised that ultimate responsibility was his. The underlying principle of his modern mindset was to recognise the value of delegating some duties to extra hands, which in turn freed up his focus for other areas. It had been tested with his team over the last year and worked so far with evident success.

He said: "Brett [Parry] does technical pads, Tony [Bryant] puts the body bag on and works the boys hard, Alastair [MacDonald] helps them out with bits and bobs of strength and conditioning, Chris [Price] helps some of the boys with their nutrition, too.

"Brett comes down on a Saturday with a couple of the boys to do pads. I might sit outside the ring because I can notice a little bit more when they're on the pads with someone else than when they're on the pads with me.

"I think it's important not to take yourself too seriously. I think a lot of coaches would never have their guys padding with anyone else but I don't take myself too seriously. Anyone who sees other people as a threat aren't confident in themselves, are they?" he suggested, in the same matter-of-fact tone that's underpins his fight philosophy.

Photos: Sacha Wiener

YAXLEY AND WARBURTON INTEND TO PUT NORTH WALES ON THE BOXING MAP
Saturday 14 December 2019

Ruthin's Sion Yaxley (5-0) and Colwyn Bay's Gerome Warburton (4-0, 1KO) were working to bring boxing shows back to North Wales.

In their latest performances, the super-welterweights fought in a suite at the Macron Stadium in Bolton. Kieran Farrell hosted frequent events in the North West of England and they were the closest in proximity to North Wales, making the connection with Yaxley and Warburton a logical link up.

Yaxley racked up his fifth win against Manchester's previously unbeaten, and erotically named, John Ardon (1-1). It came via a 40-35 decision win over four rounds. The 23-year-old, who prepared by sparring sessions with world rated super-lightweight Jack Catterall, ticked a box in his development process by facing a southpaw for the first time as a professional. It was also the first time Yaxley faced an opponent with real winning ambitions and he appreciated the challenge, easily controlling the action.

"You go in there [against a journeyman], catch them with a nice stiff jab and straight away they go on the back foot," he opened. "You know journeymen, sometimes they just come to survive, don't they? You're just going through the motions… but against someone who has come to win, it's much better. In a way, it's a breath of fresh air. I mean, because he came to win, I was landing my shots much more cleaner on him."

A right hook counterpunch put Ardon on the floor in the third round and Yaxley was evidently the better boxer. Trainer Wesley Jones was happy with the performance, a display of the skills that led Yaxley to a Welsh senior amateur title in 2018 and appearances at international tournaments. There was still plenty of progress to be made and Yaxley was self-critical in his assessment.

He said: "In the first round, it was a bit touch and go, we were both trying to figure each other out. The last 30 seconds, I picked it up and started catching him a few times. After that, it was one-way traffic, I'd say. In the last round, he was trying to throw something back, so I slipped the shot and come back with my own right hand and I dropped him. I feel I could've stopped him if I picked up the pace and proper went for it. It's all about learning at the moment, isn't it?"

Stablemate Warburton, fittingly nicknamed 'Bread Maker', came through against local debutant Scott Williams. The four rounder was scored in the Welshman's favour by the same 40-35 margin, though the extra point came from a deduction due to persistent holding rather than a knockdown. The aggressive 24-year-old attacked from the southpaw stance and Williams was made to feel uncomfortable throughout.

There have been more than 40 professional British champions from Wales but Barmouth-born Johnny Williams was the only one from the north. His heavyweight triumph over Jack Gardner in 1952 hadn't been followed for nearly 70 years. Dyffryn Boxing Club, where Yaxley and Warburton were bred since their early teenage years, was established in 1965. It had numerous medallists in the amateurs and Yaxley was determined to make memories for the region in the pro-code, too.

"The North West of England - Bolton, Manchester, Liverpool - isn't that far," said the youthful Yaxley. "But your fans come and watch you, paying good money, they're travelling a fair bit, and you want to put a show on for them. If it was in North Wales, it won't be too far and you can put on a real show for them then.

"North Wales, at the moment, is very busy. [It's] probably the best it's been in a long time, I'd say. There are plenty of places in North Wales where you can put on professional boxing shows. It'd be really nice to have something up here. You've got myself, Gerome Warburton, Osh Williams who is making his debut in a couple of weeks' time. Boxing in North Wales is on the up at the moment. It would be nice for all of us to get together and sort out a show for North Wales."

The production line from Dyffryn Boxing Club was confident it could set a trend. There hadn't been a professional show in North Wales since Tom Doran's appearance in Deeside in 2014. Both Yaxley and Warburton were managed by Sanigar Events and the Welsh-language terrestrial broadcaster S4C had expressed an interest in staging shows in North Wales.

"I'm a Welsh speaker myself, that's why Chris [Sanigar] is trying to push me on the S4C shows when he gets them," explained the bilingualist. "I think there would be massive interest to get shows in North Wales, especially if there's title fights up here as well.

"I'm yet to have a six rounder but I'm hoping my next fight will be a six rounder, if I'm honest. I'm totally ready for a six rounder and I don't think I'm far off a Welsh title. I'm quietly confident but obviously, I've just got to keep on winning and winning as I go along, isn't it?"

The next step was a return to Bolton on Saturday 14 March, another building block towards an overdue homecoming.

FOX HUNTER WILLIAMS SETS UP WORLD TITLE SHOT
Saturday 21 December 2019

Clydach's Liam Williams (22-2-1, 17KO) made a major statement and positioned himself for a world title shot by dispatching America's Alantez Fox (26-2, 12KO) in five ruthless rounds.

It was the best win of the middleweight's eight-year career and it secured a high world ranking. 'The Machine' captured the WBO Inter-Continental title and stole Queensberry's show at the Copper Box Arena in London, live on BT Sport. Williams' nasty finishing instincts extended his growing record of knockouts - all of his 14 victories over the past six years ended before the final bell.

"I don't really want to remember [what it's like to win on points]. I plan to keep going the way I have been, taking these guys out hopefully," he stated afterwards.

"People have got this image of me now like, 'Liam is a killer, he's knocking everyone over, doing this and doing that.' Unless you know me, a lot of these people fail to realise that I can actually box, as well. I can always knock them out and, if that doesn't work, I can always go to Plan B and maybe use my skillset a little bit more."

The eye-catching aggression disguised Williams' strategic intelligence. On this occasion, his plan included out-jabbing an opponent who stood at incredible six foot five inches tall and there was a sense of inevitability from the opening bell. Williams immediately found his range, tracking Fox's movement to close down the space between the pair. Being the shorter man, it was important for Williams to get close to Fox and to do it quickly, so he did it with an unexpected reverse one-two combination. Fox, after eating stinging straight shots, was forced to a neutral corner and Williams banged the body to start draining the visitor's energy tank.

Analysing how the fight started, Williams said: "Everything was part of the game plan. Everything I done, I was told to do. I was quite surprised how easy I was beating him to the jab at certain points. To be honest, the game plan was either stay well out of range or be on his chest, y'know. I just felt comfortable to exchange a couple of jabs and I came off best.

"Technically, it would've been great to box, move around him, ping him with the jab. Everyone wants to look like Muhammad Ali, don't they? Unfortunately, against an opponent such as Alantez Fox, I had to be clever about how I went about the job. It was kind of crash, bang, wallop. Put him out of his comfort zone and give it to him, that's how I had to approach it."

Williams, despite the dominance, suffered a small cut at the end of the opening round. The wound was in an awkward position below his eyebrow and called on the cutsman to keep it from deteriorating. Fox was enthused and he landed a flush right cross to start the second round. It was a brief moment of adversity for Williams and served as a reminder to stay alert and not get carried away in the heat of the moment.

"I'll be honest, I did feel it and he caught me by surprise," said Williams, honest in his recollections of an incident that many observers missed. "I think it was a good thing for me. After the first round, I thought I was going to tear through him but by landing that good shot, he didn't hurt me or have me gone, but he buzzed me a little bit, and I thought I'd better wake up. It kept me honest.

"I was aware of it [the cut]. It wasn't very much. If I'd gone to the doctor or hospital, they would've given me one or two stitches. The area where the cut was, it was in a place that when my eye was open, you couldn't even see it. Within a matter of hours, it was sealed up. It's totally disappeared now."

Williams was keen to dampen any of Fox's optimism and he forcefully reimposed himself. Fox's body language began to betray his efforts as he coped by blatantly holding Williams' arms and turning away, waiting for the referee to call for them to separate the two. Both boxers recognised Williams was the stronger man and it became obvious to everyone else in the third round. A right cross cut the bridge of Fox's nose, who took his turn to bleed in a one-sided session.

The Welshman said: "I knew I was better than him anyway because I felt so comfortable but I just thought… 'I'm hurting him so early in the fight, if I'm doing that now, what's it going to be like in three, four, five rounds time when he starts gassing?' I knew I was going to get him out of there. I tried going about it as calmly as I could but y'know what it's like when you see fighters get someone hurt, it's difficult not to go for the kill."

If Fox wasn't dazed entering the fourth round, he certainly was when he left it. 30 seconds in, Williams was in the ascendency and he detonated a series of hooks and overhands. Fox couldn't escape the onslaught and he looked weaker in his attempts to tangle with Williams' limbs. Another thumping right cross then walloped Fox to the floor and when he gawkily staggered upright. It was the cue for Williams to unleash another hurtful assault. Fox, now fully tenderised, had to use all of his awkward attributes to hear the bell.

Perhaps the indication of a perfectionist, Williams wasn't happy with all of the aspects of his work. He said: "I've watched it back a few times and I've seen a lot of things which I didn't do great but I can't complain about the performance or the win because it was a good statement. I believe I've got so much to brush up on, maybe that's me just being a bit self-critical.

"When someone's holding on to you, I just think, 'Fuck that, work!' Get whatever shots off you can. Why wait for the referee to break it? They think when they've got hold of you, the ref is going to break it and they'll have a little break, a rest for a bit. Whenever you can work, work."

Fox was clearly disorientated as he entered the fifth round and the corner could have spared him another painful attack. Referee Steve Gray issued a point deduction for repeated holding and Fox was nearly spent. Williams knew it. He rolled under Fox's attempts to hold again, launching a pair of left hooks and they sent Fox groggily tumbling to the ropes. Williams quite literally ran to his target and coldly brought the bout to a close.

"I knew he was gone because his body went really limp," said Williams, recounting the conclusion as coldly as he delivered it. "Every time he was about to go down, he'd lock on to me, even on my legs! I couldn't get a clean knockdown on him. I was buzzing him and he had a good chin, recovering quite well but every time I buzzed him, he'd wrap those big arms around me and I couldn't finish him properly."

Before the fight, Williams was ranked at #7 by the WBO and Fox occupied the #2 slot. America's Demetrius Andrade (28-0, 17KO) won the WBO title in October 2018, having previously held the super-welterweight version in 2013 and the WBA title in 2017. The 31-year-old southpaw made two successful defences of his current belt and was due to put it on the line against Ireland's daring Luke Keeler (17-2-1, 5KO) in Miami, headlining a show promoted by Eddie Hearn's Matchroom on 30 January.

Andrade's skill from the portsider stance had never been in question; doubts only came when he seemingly coasted through fights. A prime example of that bad habit came when he faced Fox on his middleweight debut in 2017. Evidently a level above, Andrade played it safe for the full duration of their 12 rounder. Fox suffered a severe shoulder injury in the second round and only had use of one arm, but Andrade stuck to his reluctant routine. It wasn't a good look and the inconsistent attention span saw Andrade knocked to the floor, too.

Williams was mindful that comparisons would be made when he faced Fox. He said: "I definitely planned to go and do a better job [than Andrade]. If it didn't come, I was prepared. Leading up to the fight, I thought it could turn out to be difficult because he's been 12 [rounds] with Andrade. I knew I'd better be prepared for a long night but I planned to do a better job and I grabbed people's imagination.

"Andrade is obviously good, a southpaw and awkward. He's got good boxing ability and I think he carries decent power but the same as my other opponents, I believe I can beat him. I've got enough power to trouble any of these middleweights and he'll be the same as any other opponent. If I hit him on the chin, he can go.

"At one point, I fought three southpaws in a short space of time. I knocked one of them out in the first and the other two in the second round. I actually get on really well with southpaws. I just like a different challenge sometimes, because I can get a bit stale. If I haven't got something to work towards with different game plans and different styles, I do get a bit fed up. I'd rather a bigger challenge."

Williams was well aware of the champion's abilities, and so was his trainer Dominic Ingle. Stablemate Billy Joe Saunders was due to defend the WBO title against Andrade, when he was mandatory challenger himself, in 2018. However, Saunders was ruled out when he tested positive for the stimulant oxilofrine in a random VADA doping test. The Massachusetts State Athletic Commission refused to license Saunders, who insisted it was taken through a common decongestant nasal spray, and he subsequently vacated the title. Andrade went on to win it by dropping late replacement Walter Kuatondokwa numerous times, before fizzing out and settling for a typically cautious decision win.

All throughout the build-up to Williams' thrashing of Fox, it was advertised as a 'final' eliminator for Andrade and the winner was promised mandatory challenger status. However, the WBO President Francisco Varcarcel was quick to clarify that pole position for the winner wasn't actually guaranteed. It was still likely Williams would challenge Andrade in 2020, especially as the champion hadn't faced a mandatory challenger since winning the belt two years ago. Frank Warren, who promoted Williams, enjoyed a notoriously healthy relationship with the Puerto Rican-based WBO as he was one of the first mainstream promoters to utilise the organisation when it was established in 1988. The two parties had a long history together and it benefitted five Welsh world champions; Robbie Regan, Barry Jones, Joe Calzaghe, Enzo Maccarinelli and Nathan Cleverly.

The fight against Fox was Williams' fifth under Dominic Ingle and their relationship appeared to be going from strength to strength. They trained together at the infamous Wincobank Gym and Williams lived in the Chapeltown area of Sheffield during training camps. The move reduced home comforts and any temptations on offer to Williams at home in Wales, where he had trained with Gary Lockett. The previous set up was very successful before the two losses to Liam Smith in 2017. Even then, Williams was winning the first fight until referee Terry O'Connor missed head butt that caused a cut and obliged the corner to pull him out. However, Williams felt the sacrifice of moving to Sheffield was more than showing its worth.

"I don't even think I'd still be boxing if I didn't move away. I was getting so fed up with it, so many things dragging me here, there and everywhere, I couldn't focus on what I needed to do. People asking me to go out, people asking me to go for food, I didn't know if I'm coming or going. I just wanted to focus.

"It's been five fights with him [Ingle] now and five stoppages. Everything is going perfect and I couldn't ask for better. I feel very confident with Dom in the corner. I feel he's got a really calming thing about him and he never panics if he's in a sticky situation. He's got his way with words and I feel we're ready for the big fights now. We'll just see what comes next."

HARRIS' CHANCE FOR DREAM WORLD TITLE CONFIRMED
Friday 3 January 2020

If getting a world title shot was a New Year's resolution for Jay Harris (17-0, 9KO), the flyweight didn't have to wait long for it to come true.

Just days into 2020, it was announced that the Swansea native would cross the Atlantic to challenge Julio Cesar Martinez (15-1, 12KO), the WBC world champion, on Matchroom's show at the Ford Center in Frisco, Texas in February. Harris was on holiday when it was offered and he didn't hesitate to accept the offer, once he eventually found out about it.

"I was in Disneyland Paris and my battery died on my phone," he explained. "I came back to the hotel, put the charger in and turned it on. My phone was going mental. My father was saying 'ring me, ring me', so I rang my father and he was like, 'we've got the shot!' I told my girlfriend and my daughter. It was unreal.

"In a heartbeat, I took it straight away. I wasn't even doubting it, like. As soon as they told me, I was like 'yeah! It's a world title shot, I've got to take it.' It's the highest thing [in boxing] and it's the WBC, the one [title] everyone wants."

Martinez rose to fame over his last three eventful outings; upsetting Andrew Selby at altitude in Mexico in March, bending Charlie Edwards' ribs and the rulebook in a strange 'no decision' in August, before breaking down ex-title holder Cristofer Rosales to finally become world champion in December. All three opponents struggled to cope with Martinez's relentless style and marauding attacks. Jabs were rarely used, instead their absence was compensated by persistent barrages of heavy hooks. Harris paid credit to the results, but he believed there were mitigating factors involved.

"He is a good fighter. He wouldn't be world champion if he wasn't good, would he?" said Harris, aware of what awaited him. "As a fighter, he's a very strong fighter and obviously he can hit but I think I'm more than capable of beating him, see.

"His stance is all-wrong. He's not very good at switching, he tries to switch but he's not very good. He relies a lot on his power. He must hit [hard], obviously, because he's stopped 12 of the 15 people he's won against. I've got to make myself very wary of his left hand."

Martinez's storming form came under the supervision of Eddy Reynoso, trainer of superstar Saul 'Canelo' Alvarez, and it led to a deal with Eddie Hearn. Like forgoers Joe Calzaghe and Nathan Cleverly, Harris was trained by his father. Peter Harris won domestic titles in his day and the team knew the game plan would be crucial. Harris owned a slight height advantage and he was also an effective body puncher. He believed those attributes could, in parts, match Martinez's ferocious physicality.

"When you see me in the ring against Angel Moreno [UD12] and Paddy Barnes [TKO4], I looked twice the size of both of them," studied Harris. "I'm a big flyweight and I feel strong at the weight. We're going to have to test how strong he is.

"Of course, there's going to be a game plan. We're going to work a lot on my footwork mainly, getting in and out, away from trouble. Just box him, I know I can box. I think I'm a much better boxer than him, as well. When he wants to work, get away and when he doesn't want to work, put the pressure on him. One of his early fights, the one he lost, it was only four rounds but the boy put it on him and kind of broke his heart."

From 1914 to 2020, 13 Welsh boxers had achieved the ultimate goal and claimed legitimate world honours. Ystrad Mynach's Lauren Price, the only amongst the group to win a world title as an amateur, was also the only boxer to do it outside of the UK. Gwent light-heavyweights Joe Calzaghe and Nathan Cleverly won respective Ring Magazine and WBA 'Regular' belts on the road, though neither honour had official recognition. Harris spent most of his career touring venues across the country; it gave him a flavour of fighting on the road and an adjustable attitude.

He said: "I'm not afraid to go away. I'd say this to anybody. I know I'm going over there as a massive underdog but I thrive off that a little bit because there's not a lot of pressure on me. There's bags of pressure on him, they're building him up to be a superstar. To be honest, I don't think he is. It'll be a fantastic thing to be the first Welshman to win [a legitimate world title] away, especially in the US.

"I was the away fighter [in his last fight]. Paddy [Barnes] was the golden boy, wasn't he? A very loud crowd but I've always said this; it's only me and him [the opponent] in the ring at the end of the day. There's no one else. I know the crowd is going to play a massive part; they're going to be loud. I don't know if there are a lot of Mexicans in Texas, I haven't got a clue to be honest but it's the same as any other fight, just this one is for a WBC world title."

Since signing an agreement to join MTK Global's ever-expanding umbrella in February 2019, Harris got going in a routine outing, then captured continental titles and then set himself up for a world title. The turnaround in fortunes was reward for his persistence; it was well known Harris overcame inactivity and a chronic lack of promotional backing earlier in his career. However familiar that storyline can be in Welsh boxing, what made Harris special was that he came through it all and now stood on the brink of a childhood dream. The work ethic was an example to others going through the same struggle and the experience made Harris exceptionally hungry to succeed.

"18 months ago, I was on the verge of quitting," he revealed, now removed from the dismay. "Thankfully, the good team around me and my family persuaded me not to. I had a good think to myself. I thought 'I've been doing this way too long to give it up.' The 'no quit' desire has got me this far. Fair dos to MTK, they've changed everything for me. They've honoured what they said. Timing is everything and I do believe it's my time. It has to be. Hopefully, people will look back at this story and stick at the sport."

At this point, Harris had been a professional boxer for over six and a half years. During that whole time, he sandwiched training sessions around shifts as a forklift driver in a warehouse for online retailer Amazon. His progression as a puncher afforded him the flexibility to reduce his hours, especially when fight night neared, and he enjoyed the luxury of being a full time fighter ahead of the Martinez fight. The tougher times kept Harris grounded and enhanced his appreciation of the opportunities finally coming his way.

He said: "I've had a word with Amazon and they're fully onboard to give me the full two months off, which is fantastic. So, I can fully focus on the fight. It's brilliant by them and I've got a couple of good sponsors on board now, so everything is ticking over lovely, as it goes.

"As soon as it got announced, I was like 'right, I need to get a meeting in.' I got a meeting with the boss and as soon as I went in, he was like 'what can we do to help you? Do you want us to pay for flights to go over there?' They asked if my girlfriend wanted time off. I just said, 'look, I just really need time off for this fight, it's very important.' It was done.

"I've got no worries. I don't have to worry about going to work on Thursday or Friday. I can get good sleep, good rest. It does make a hell of a difference."

With a world title shot scheduled, Harris made the decision to vacate his European title six months after beating Spain's Moreno. The decision came as the EBU insisted on a defence against Italy's capable Mohammed Obbadi (21-1, 13KO). It wouldn't have been practically possible on the Welshman's calendar, yet it could have suited another. It opened an opportunity for Barry's Andrew Selby (13-1, 7KO) as the EBU has ordered him to be the other party in a vacant title fight. There was little news of Selby's plans, only that he'd vacated his British title and reportedly left trainer Daniel Chapman to rejoin Tony Borg.

A win for Harris against Martinez would secure his place in Welsh boxing history, as well as Swansea's sporting folklore. Gorseinon's Colin Jones came within a whisker of a world title in 1983 and Bonymaen's Enzo Maccarinelli then made the breakthrough in 2006, reigning as WBO cruiserweight champion for two years. 29-year-old Harris kept a relatively low-profile life away from boxing. His spare time was spent following his beloved Swansea City FC, or with his friends and family. There would be a new addition to the family in the coming months as Harris and his partner Lesley welcome a second child, providing all the inspiration he needed to confront Martinez.

Photo: Spencer Love

WELSH AREA COUNCIL HONOUR AWARD WINNERS
Friday 31 January 2020

The BBBoC Welsh Area Council held its annual awards to honour Welsh boxers of the past and present.

The dinner event at the Marriot Hotel in Cardiff was into its fourth year, established as one of the highlights of the Welsh boxing calendar. It acted as a celebration of the year that has passed and curtain raiser for what lay ahead.

Clydach's Liam Williams collected the ceremony's most prestigious honour, 'Boxer of the Year.' BBBoC Steward Ron Pavett presented it in recognition of a hat-trick of knockout wins in 2019. 'The Machine' hit career best form with; a British title defence against Joe Mullender (KO2), WBC Silver title win against Karim Anchor (KO2) and WBO Inter-Continental title win against Alantez Fox (KO5). All three were highlight reel finishes and set Williams up for an assault on the world scene.

"It was my best year in boxing, I would say and I'm pretty sure most people would say it, too," considered Williams. "I'm in the gym with Dom Ingle now and it feels like I've just gone there yesterday [for the first time]. Everything is still as exciting and fresh. I believe last year was just the start for me and the next couple of years, I'm going to keep building. I genuinely feel like I'm getting better. Each fight camp, I seem to be more switched on and dedicated the older I'm getting. I'm a bit more wise, y'know."

The swell of success earned Williams a high world ranking and after receiving the BBBoC award, the middleweight also received a mounted painting from Patrick J Killian. The world-renowned artist boxed for Cwmbran and Wales as an amateur and his latest portrait took pride of place in Williams' new home. Swansea's Jay Harris and Cardiff's Joe Cordina were deservedly nominated, too.

He said: "Looking back, I was probably moved a little bit fast [early in his career]. I got to a stage where I was still learning on the job but I was too far ahead of myself to be able to turn back and stop the clock. I got myself into a position where I had to keep pushing forward. I do believe my losses and my setbacks have moulded me into the man and fighter I am.

"I've realised I can't fiddle my way through and become a champion just off talent and a little bit of grit. Sometimes you've got to put yourself in uncomfortable positions and sometimes do things you don't really want to do to get the best of yourself. That's exactly what I'm doing."

Tonypandy's Rhys Edwards, a neighbour of Williams, was awarded with 'Prospect of the Year.' The featherweight chalked up seven wins in 2019 and did so in style, boosting his reputation across the British boxing landscape. A three-course meal was served and Edwards skipped dessert, staying dedicated to his duties ahead of an upcoming step-up against Johnny Phillips. Ammanford's Jake Anthony and Cardiff's Maredudd Thomas were also in contention.

"I'm really, really pleased for him [Edwards]. Speaking from experience, when you're from the same area, people don't wanna see someone coming up through the ranks who is as good as them. It's quite sad to see," said Williams, who lived a handful of hills away from his fellow Rhondda boxer. "I remember Rhys coming in the gym when he didn't even box. I was young myself, lets say I was 13 and he was like five or six. He was with Mansel [Edwards – father] and I remember him knocking out loads of pull ups and press ups.

"I was thinking, 'this kid is a beast. Where did he come from?' I remember him being a little tank as a kid, that's my first memory of him. He's a good kid and the talent, it's serious talent. If he has dedication to go with it, which I believe he has, I'm really excited for him. He's a class act and he's going to do really well."

'Contest of the Year' was shared between Cardiff's Joe Cordina and Trelewis' Gavin Gwynne. They previously shared 12 competitive rounds for the British title and Cordina prevailed in an entertaining affair in the summer. It was the first time two Welshmen had met for a British title in 25 years and the significance of the fight, whilst both were undefeated, was also cited.

Chris Jenkins' dramatic upset of British welterweight champion Johnny Garton and Jay Harris' European triumph against Angel Moreno were also nominated for 'Contest of the Year.' However, Harris' four round thumping of Paddy Barnes in Belfast and Kristian Touze's Welsh title war with Angelo Dragone went without recognition by the decision-makers. The oversights were odd.

Pat Thomas received a 'Services to Boxing Award.' After moving from the West Indies to settle in Cardiff, Thomas overcame poverty to become a two-weight British champion in the 1970s. Thomas would later train future world champion Barry Jones and he was still devoted to the sport, instrumental for his local boxing club in Butetown, Tiger Bay ABC.

Officials from the BBBoC's Welsh Area Council fittingly paid tribute to two boxers no longer with us. Heavyweight Jack Petersen and flyweight Dai Dower won numerous titles in the 1930s and 1950s, respectively, and were posthumously welcomed to the Welsh Boxing Hall of Fame for their achievements. Petersen and Dower took their places amongst a select group of history makers.

Photo: Liam Hartery

QUALIFYING OPPORTUNITIES CONFIRMED FOR TRIO OF OLYMPIC HOPEFULS
Thursday 6 February 2020

Caldicot's welterweight Rosie Eccles and Ystrad Mynach's middleweight Lauren Price ventured stateside as preparation for upcoming Olympic qualifiers was taken to a new level.

They were part of a squad of Team GB hopefuls who endured a 10 day training camp at the United States Olympic Training Centre in Colorado Springs. The high-altitude region made it the perfect place to test their bodies to the limit and Price and Eccles did just that. Greeted by 'home of the brave' slogans plastered on the walls of the gym, Team GB were quickly reminded of their roles and they made the most of their surroundings. An extreme training routine included lung-busting cardio sessions in oxygen-reduced conditions and regular spars with rivals from USA Boxing.

"The altitude was the biggest challenge for me and my breathing. They [Team USA] were fighting the week after, so they were match fit. We were just going back in and weren't conditioned to it," assessed Eccles, having now recovered her breath. "I'd like it if the air was a bit easier to breathe, it nearly killed me. I'm a pressure fighter and a puncher, so it took the edge off me to say the least. It was a good camp, good to get away.

"We had different [types of] training. We had two days where we sparred longer rounds, sometimes with three different partners, and then we had technical spars, which I'm not really a fan of. And then gym bouts come with a bit more pressure, so it's three rounds, like a fight in the gym and you're in the main ring and people are watching. You have your slot, no one scores it and it's not judged but you have a coach in there as a ref. They can get tasty, there's a bit of an edge to them and it brings that competition pressure."

More important than an opportunity to make memories, the trip was intended to take the boxers out of their comfort zones and away from their base at the English Institute of Sport in Sheffield. However, they would enjoy some home comforts when they next entered the ring. 13 boxers would be selected to represent Team GB at their first Olympic qualifier, scheduled for

London's Copper Box Arena on 14-24 March. The places were divided between eight weights for men and five for women.

Eager for the occasion, Eccles said: "People always ask me 'when are you fighting next?' or 'when are you fighting in this country?' I never know when I'm fighting in Wales or Britain, so just to be fighting in front of a home crowd when people can come watch... actually, it's kind of unbelievable already how many people are messaging me and wanting tickets. It's nice to be on home turf and not have to travel. I hate flying and it'll also be that extra bit of motivation."

Price, the recently crowned world champion, and Eccles weren't the only Welsh boxers with a chance to qualify. Swansea's Sammy Lee, who endured his own gruelling camp in Kazakhstan, was selected to join them. The 21-year-old shot onto the scene by winning youth and senior Commonwealth Games gold medals in 2017 and 2018, respectively. Having dropped from light-heavyweight to middleweight, the southpaw's selection could gatecrash the Olympics much earlier than expected. Eccles knew Lee inside out and had long-been a believer in their collective ability to represent Wales on the world stage.

"In a way, we've grown up together over the last three or four years. We were living in these little rooms in Sport Wales for two years leading up to the [2014] Commonwealth Games and we got on Team GB at around the same time," she recalled with considerable vigour. "I feel very proud that it's the three of us and it's really nice for Colin Jones [head coach of the Welsh national team] and the coaching team there that they've really brought us to GB and we can go on to bring back Olympic medals. Three Olympic medals would be very special. Just having three of us at the Olympics would be a first.

"Me and Sammy, we're not massive on social media. I've purposely quieted down because I'd rather let my boxing do the talking. Sammy isn't too dissimilar either and people forget what he's done," said Eccles in reference their relatively low public profiles. "In a lot of places [since the Commonwealth Games], he's been unlucky and now he's dropped a weight and I think he's going to do something exciting.

"For me, it's a two-fold dream. I've always dreamt of being an Olympian and I've also dreamt about being an Olympic champion. So, it's like one stage at a time. None of us are just happy to turn up, it's not in our nature. We're not really participants, we're winners. That's the same for all three of us."

The last three Olympic cycles in Beijing 2008, London 2012 and Rio 2016 were Team GB's most successful for 50 years. The prospect of three Welsh boxers at the 2020 Olympics in Tokyo would be history making in itself. To achieve that, the trio would have to reach the semi-finals of their qualifier or be the best losing quarter-finalist, proving the latter with a box off.

Tokyo 2020 would be the third consecutive Olympic Games to feature women boxing and it would also be the first to feature five weight categories – extended from three at London and Rio. Eccles was a beneficiary of that change and women's boxing was evidently making progress. After its inclusion as a demonstration sport in 1904, women's boxing was outlawed across continents until the International Boxing Association [AIBA] finally permitted it in 1993. It soared in popularity in recent times and the infrastructure had been catching up.

Eccles, a university graduate, said: "When I won my first European medal [2016], I was at 64KG and I couldn't go on Team GB simply due to the fact that it wasn't an Olympic weight. I sat in the middle of a 15KG gap, there was no chance I was making 60KG [lightweight] and there's no chance I'm a 75KG [middleweight] fighter. It was the same for other girls. I'm not a massive at 69KG [welterweight], I weigh about 2KG less when I fight. 69KG will be booming because of the massive gap, whereas before you saw boxers who were cooked at the weight below. Now you see new weights emerging and it shows what talent is out there. I think it's really exciting for women's boxing."

Selection for the qualifier also represented a significant show of faith in Eccles by the Team GB decision-makers. Eccles and England's Sandy Ryan had been locked in an intense rivalry for almost four years. It began when Ryan handed Eccles her first ever defeat in 2016, a time when Ryan owned over 100 bouts of experience compared to Eccles' 13 bouts. They met again in the finals of the Commonwealth Games in 2018, where Ryan took a see-saw decision and then Eccles finally made her mark with a win at the 2019 European Championships. The pecking order switched, especially when Eccles went further in the recent World Championships, and she entered 2020 with reason to be confident that she was top of the tree at Team GB. Selection for the qualifier confirmed it, at least for the time being, and Eccles credited the rivalry for her development.

"The thing with me and Sandy, it's really… interesting," said Eccles, doing her best impression of a disinclined diplomat. "When I joined Team GB just after the Commonwealth Games, going in I was the fresh face. How do I establish myself there? It did feel like a big uphill battle.

"I've been chipping away and I was really hoping to draw her in the European Championships and lucky enough, I did what I needed to do out there. Getting my hand raised was like 'finally!'

"There's naturally a lot of tension. We both want the same thing and we've gone from being in separate camps to the same camp. For me, it's been a massive motivator and I think, with it being my first ever loss and how the Commonwealth final went, that's why I've been so determined.

"We live in separate houses and we're not mates. We're never going to be friends. We're very different people to begin with and on top of that we want what each other's dream is and only one can have it. It's a tough environment because you constantly face 'that person' but I do think it's made me tougher, having such a close rivalry. Some of the gaps [in the squad] are more obvious but for me, it's been a big push on and it's given me resilience I need."

Amateur boxing on the international stage had long been the subject of widespread criticism. Suspicion had repeatedly haunted AIBA, especially around its finances, governance and officiating, for years. The International Olympic Committee [IOC] suspended the governing body from its position in May 2019, a decision that threatened the very presence of boxing at the Olympics. The IOC then appointed a special Boxing Task Force [BTF] to take charge of the situation and the five international qualifiers were the first major opportunity to demonstrate their competence.

Whilst AIBA's controversies were a well-recognised threat to amateur boxing, another legitimate threat to the Olympics was completely unexpected. The Asian and Oceania qualifying events were moved from Wuhan, China to Amman, Jordan due to the breakout of COVID-19. The respiratory virus infected and killed tens of thousands of people in China - the world's most populated country with over a billion inhabitants. COVID-19 coincidentally originated in Wuhan, approximately 1,500 miles away from Tokyo, and started to spread worldwide.

At this stage, the COVID-19 situation was still developing – much like Olympic qualification for Price, Eccles and Lee.

FIXED FIGHT? BETTING CONTROVERSY OVERSHADOWS DARCH DEFEAT
Saturday 8 February 2020

When Dorian Darch (12-12-1, 1KO) was stopped in three rounds by Doncaster's David Allen (18-5-2, 15KO), it was supposed to be yet another typically predictable fight to inflate the record of a well-known boxer in the home corner.

It wasn't the main event of Matchroom's show at the Sheffield Arena, or even the chief support, but the post-fight reaction created more media headlines than any other fight on a show that featured former IBF world welterweight champion Kell Brook.

Darch, a heavyweight from Aberdare, was felled in the third round, an unsurprising outcome given the context of his form. The 35-year-old was winless since 2016 and had been stopped seven times in that period, which was spent travelling the country to take on its best prospects. The results were partly due to receiving late notice and a recurring bicep injury, but also because sometimes Darch was booked to fight a level or two above his ability.

The latter was likely to be the explanation for the way the Allen fight ended but it was the peculiar way it played out that sparked scrutiny and some farfetched calls of a 'fix.' 27-year-old Allen had been open about his severe gambling addiction and that red flag led to some observers raising an eyebrow when bookmakers reported irregular betting activity in the hours leading up to the fight. It was reported that a significant amount of money was staked specifically on the third round.

Allen's antics on social media, usually self-deprecating anecdotes, had amassed an army of online fans, termed 'casuals' by more hardcore loyalists. His excessive clowning masked a reluctance to train for most of his career and the 'White Rhino' had been exposed when he stepped up against boxers who prepare properly. Still, he'd shown brief glimpses of talent beyond Darch's level and indicated he should win some domestic titles. That was why fans were surprised to see Darch fight on even terms so comfortably in the first and second rounds.

Cornered by Andrew Morgan from Mountain Ash Boxing Club, Darch pushed out a consistent jab and his flicks found Allen's face far more than they should have. It was around this point that the Sky Sports commentary team informed the television audience that Darch and Allen shared breakfast together, another bad look in the eyes of sceptics. Allen moved a lot, posing with his hands low and switching to southpaw to pass the time. In between half-hearted digs to the body, Allen spent most of his energy leaning from the waist in an extended feeling out process. Darch appeared to take it slightly more seriously and worked away with right hands in the second round to catch Allen as he slowly swayed from side to side.

"The first round, he was making me miss and being defensive, flicking out the odd jab. In the second round, I was connecting, everything was going alright," said Darch, who was happy to take advantage of Allen's lethargic start. "I've watched it back and I thought I did win round two. I think he might've been cruising. Don't get me wrong, he could've put his foot on the gas at any point but in my mind, in the ring, I was doing alright."

It was relatively light touch work from both men but that can be easily explained. Darch knew he was unlikely to win, even if he deserved it, and if he upped the pace, it risked giving Allen a chance to take him out. It was a sad, but accepted, indictment of the way professional boxing operates in some circumstances. On the other hand, it was Allen's first fight since a severe beating from Liverpool's David Price and he was understandably gun shy, even stating his desire to ease through the scheduled six rounds until the final bell at the pre-fight press conference.

Jason Shinfield, who led the Yorkshireman's corner, called Allen 'lazy' and implored for more impact. Allen responded instantly and landed a solid right cross seconds into the third round. A triplet of left hooks to the ribs followed and Darch quickly covered his body to leave his head exposed. Allen spotted the opening and switched his attention upstairs, with a left hook to momentarily freeze Darch in his tracks. The Welshman was then tumbled over and got back to his feet by the time referee John Latham reached the count of eight.

A two-fisted attack followed and the only place for Darch to escape was the canvas. He lay flat on his back with his feet in the air before slowly sitting up, shaking his head and accepting he wouldn't be able to win. The stoppage also meant the BBBoC issued Darch with a mandatory 28-day suspension. That cancelled his plans for another fight in February, which was ignored by many of the conspiracy theorists on social media.

The stoppage was sudden and a contrast to the earlier action, though that's the nature of boxing; things can change quickly and Darch had a simple explanation for the ending: "He [Allen] had a bollocking at the end of the second round off Eddie Hearn and his cornermen. That riled him up and he come out in the third round all guns blazing. He caught me with a left hook and it was just one of them things."

Shortly after the fight, the BBBoC confirmed an investigation had been opened by the Gambling Commission, an independent non-departmental public body funded by the Department for Digital, Culture, Media and Sport [DCMS]. The Gambling Commission remained tight lipped in their public statement: "We don't comment on ongoing investigations or confirm they exist because doing so could harm any investigation or could unjustifiably damage reputations. We may comment on a case after its conclusion but many cases are led by other bodies including sports governing bodies or law enforcement agencies."

Darch found out about the investigation two days later. The civil engineer was driving to work on Monday morning when a friend sent him a screenshot of a story in a newspaper. Privy to the truth, he was initially relaxed about the opinions of fans, until he realised the potential consequences that mass media coverage could have on his family.

"I laughed it off. I'm just lucky that my daughter is only six because it could've affected her if she sees it printed all over the papers with no truth behind it. A lot of boxing fans, particularly people who watch Dave Allen because he's Twitter famous… they don't know anything about boxing. They watch because he's funny on Twitter. Then they jump on the bandwagon as soon as someone mentions something [like a fix]. They're talking shit. I'd like to see them get hit on the chin by someone who is 19st and get back up."

The first part of Darch's career saw him amass 12 wins from 16 fights. It included an appearance against Anthony Joshua in 2014 and Darch managed to stay on his feet against the Olympic gold medallist. Joshua would go on to unify three of the world heavyweight titles in Cardiff and Darch went on the road, using boxing to fund family holidays.

Holding a full-time job in construction and raising a family understandably hindered the Welshman's ability to be 'fight fit' but he promised one last farewell fight. After that, Darch planned to embark on a future away from the ring.

EDWARDS STEPS UP IN STYLE TO SEE-OFF PHILLIPS
Saturday 15 February 2020

Tonypandy's rising talent Rhys Edwards (10-0, 4KO) passed his first step up in style by dominating Surrey's Jonny Phillips (5-4, 2KO) over six rounds at London's York Hall.

Gary Lockett guided the 19-year-old since he turned professional and wanted him to 'grow up' as the stakes heightened. Edwards responded by literally moving into the gym to live for spells of his training camp. It enabled the featherweight to fully commit to training by day and relax away from any distractions by night, albeit on a camp bed.

Edwards was sure he'd done enough for a whitewash, but he was denied when referee Kieran McCann someway found a round in favour of Phillips. To the bemusement of everyone, the official surprisingly judged it 59-55. It wasn't the first time things didn't go as they should have on the day. At the weigh-in, Phillips came in nearly three pounds over the agreed limit.

"I was quite tamping with the referee giving him a round. No offence to Jonny but I wouldn't give him a minute of any round," Edwards justifiably protested. "I was gutted he gave him a point because [world title challenger] Stephen Smith won all six rounds [against Phillips] and I didn't want to do worse than him. It is what it is, I know I didn't lose a round."

Phillips shot across the ring straight away, pushing forward with his head and it took less than 15 seconds for the physical tactics to be disciplined. He quickly abandoned the reckless approach, trying to box with Edwards and he was second best. Edwards danced around the target and navigated Phillips to the ropes with a consistent jab. It was a fast start, the highlights came when Edwards staggered Phillips with a left hook and short uppercuts through the middle.

The occasion, atop a Priority Boxing show, was a test of Edwards' composure and his attitude was positive. Phillips grew erratic in the second round and Edwards' jab repeatedly thwarted those speculative attacks, which kept it at arm's length. The pace settled in the third round and Phillips spent more time on the back foot. When he did respond, Edwards tucked up to catch hooks and counter in the pocket, before his movement reset the routine.

There was increasing purchase on Edwards' punches, especially in the screw shots that were whipped up from his waist to pelt Phillips' forehead. For a natural counterpuncher, Edwards was just as effective in his proactive work and he sapped Phillips' energy with body shots in the fourth round. The youngster was told he was 'just a kid' in the build-up and he took delight in disproving the label.

Edwards sat down on his shots in the fifth round, loading a crisp uppercut with enough power to send Phillips' gum-shield to the other side of the ring. Phillips remained game throughout and was still trying in the sixth round, rallying when he had chances to come forward. Edwards' ability always had the answer and he finished the fight by shooting right cross counters over the top of jabs that came his way. The Welshman signalled to a vocal crowd at the final bell, having extinguished Phillips' ambition whenever it flickered.

"I knew he didn't have the skills to beat me, he was always going to try to brawl and rough me up. As soon as he came with his head, I knew to move or tuck up, take what he had and come back," said Edwards in his synopsis. "I don't know where they [opponents] get the idea from that I'm just a kid. I know I'm young but obviously I'm no push over. I don't fight like a kid, I fight like a man, so look out in two years.

"As an amateur, I was always kind of, as they say, running and counter punching. I'd never catch shots and come back. That's something I've learned with Gary and, to be honest, I've picked it up so quickly you'd swear I'd been a pro for years. The amount I've improved in a year is crazy. It's down to Gary training me and making me a more composed fighter."

Phillips, a beatable but very respectable opponent, presented the perfect task to complete Edwards' apprenticeship. The Englishman had been a real handful against other prospects, such as Cardiff's Jacob Robinson, justifying his confidence in causing an upset. The occasion concluded the first chapter of Edwards' professional career. Until now, the prospect had faced relatively low risk opposition, allowing him to learn small lessons on the job. The hurdle was higher for this fight and it was cleared with plenty of space to spare.

Evaluating his progress and potential next steps, Edwards said: "The show was great. The atmosphere between my fans and his fans was a great. I really enjoyed it. All my fans singing was really good. I had a bit of a step up in my 10th fight against Jonny Phillips and I felt good in there. To be honest, I wouldn't like to box anymore terrible journeymen. I'd like to keep the level of Jonny or step it up again. I'm open to titles.

"I'd be happy to move to an eight rounder in my next fight but that's not down to me, it's down to Gary. He's in charge. I just do as he says, really. I'm just going to listen to Gary; keep learning, keep improving and keep winning."

Edwards' immediate plans included a short holiday to Malta and then a trip stateside, to Texas, in support of Swansea's Jay Harris. The talents had struck a friendship through regular sparring at Llanrumney Boxing Club and Edwards had to be there in person to cheer on Harris' world title challenge.

Earlier in the night, Cardiff's Fred Evans (7-1) came through a tougher than expected encounter with Wilmer Gonzalez (20-17-1, 13KO). Like Edwards, the Olympic silver medallist earned a 59-55 decision win, albeit in completely contrasting circumstances.

Gonzalez was a Nicaraguan based in Spain and a frequent visitor to away corners across the UK. He arrived seven pounds overweight, much to the annoyance of Evans and his team, and made that count in spurts during their six rounder at super-middleweight.

Evans found the target early and landed his jab through Gonzalez's low guard. It sent spray from his hair and Evans was happy in the opener. Right hooks followed and it was evident Gonzalez felt the shots, despite the unconvincing showmanship. Gonzalez was warned by the referee for careless positioning of his head and that interrupted Evans' work. He followed that with wild lunges, attempting to stifle Evans' skills and it disturbed the Welshman.

A couple of left crosses at the end of the third round sent Gonzalez stumbling to the ropes and the favour was returned back to Evans in the fourth round. Evans received his fair share of solid shots and he appeared buzzed. It was a cause for concern in the corner and it energised Gonzalez's levels of confidence.

There were more warning signs in the fifth round when Gonzalez landed successive overhands. Evans collected himself by circling the ring and his southpaw jabs looked for openings to regain the upper hand. A quieter phase followed in the sixth round and it allowed Evans to recover. He remained more consistent but swung wide shots that his corner advised against. It brought a close an uncomfortable evening.

Photo: Huw Fairclough

DRAINED DAVIES SUFFERS DEFEAT TO INSPIRED SADIQ

Saturday 22 February 2020

The plan was for Pontllanfraith's Kody Davies (10-1, 3KO) to drop a weight division and build towards domestic titles but an ambitious experiment with the scales backfired and left London's inspired Umar Sadiq (10-1, 6KO) on hand to capitalise.

The scorecards for the British title eliminator were 98-92, 97-93 and 96-94 in favour of Sadiq and there were few complaints when it was announced. The former accountant was far more energetic in his home city and, crucially, in the super-middleweight division as he set a blistering pace for the full 10 rounds.

"I don't want to say too much and make too much out of it..." divulged Davies, aware that boxing is beset with anecdotes about boxers struggling to lose weight. "It was very hard work and I had to sacrifice a lot.

"It was always a question in the back of my mind; whether I can make it [super-middleweight], whether I can perform at that weight, whether I can pursue my career at that weight. I decided to give it a go. Obviously, it didn't come out the way we wanted it to, so I'll go back to light-heavyweight and pick up from there."

Frustratingly, Davies was at the same venue five months earlier and had already won an eliminator at light-heavyweight. However, his unanimous decision over Zak Chelli didn't amount to much in the eyes of the BBBoC, who ordered a fight between Craig Richards and Shakan Peters for the British title vacated by Joshua Buatsi.

Davies said: "I think my promoter could've done more, a lot of people could've done more to get me in that circle of names to be called up for a British title fight. I won a British title eliminator, and I know you can go on and have a final eliminator, but the bottom line is, I boxed in a British title eliminator and I was no closer to a British title than before the fight. It didn't make sense really."

There was no doubt that Davies looked aesthetically impressive on the scales but behind closed doors, the drop from 175lbs to 168lbs put a serious strain on his body. The 25-year-old made a weight he hadn't seen since his teens and the 30 hours between the weigh-in and the fight wasn't enough time to refuel. To put it into a wider context, Davies was a muscular heavyweight as an amateur, weighing well over 200lbs as recently as 30 months earlier. He didn't need hindsight to know everything had to go perfectly when dealing with such fine margins but Davies admitted to unknowingly scoring a critical own goal.

"I don't think there's anybody else on the planet who has dropped 25 kilograms [55lbs]. We tried it out, me and Gavin [Rees – trainer], we did everything perfectly up until the weigh-in. After the weigh-in, I started eating junk. I shouldn't have, I should've kept it clean up until after I boxed. I overloaded my body with fluid and junk food and I think that paid dividends in the fight. It just wasn't my night," said Davies, the statement tinged with a tone of confession.

"I don't regret it. I trained to make super-middleweight, it was obviously a step too far. I learned that in the fight. Thankfully, I didn't get hurt with nothing but I found out I'm a natural light-heavyweight. That's where I'm going to carry out the rest of my career."

Davies and Sadiq fought on even terms in the early rounds. Both boxed at mid-range and tried to work their way in without risking too much. The Welshman was the first to make his mark, unloading hooks when Sadiq squared up on the ropes. Soon after in the second round, Sadiq sent a series of long single shots towards Davies, who was reduced to throwing in short spells. Sadiq seemed aware that he couldn't win a fencing match and he upped the ante in the third round. His activity increased and it gave Davies the opportunity to land a heavy southpaw hook but that success was short lived. Sadiq was undeterred and stuck to his tactics, even when Davies took a step back to create space for some solid body shots in the fourth round.

Davies said: "After the fourth round, I was just fucked, I couldn't do much else. I hoped for the best but it didn't come off. As devastating as it was at the time, I'm over it now. A lot of people have been saying that up until the end of the fourth round, I was looking okay but I can tell you now, from the minute I woke up that morning, I knew it was going to be a tough night. I was doing some pads in the changing rooms, I was absolutely fucked then and my legs were like cement."

Only a brief warning to avoid head clashes interrupted the pair in the middle rounds. Sadiq wasn't the most accurate puncher but he didn't stop occupying Davies' attention, reversing any momentum that could be gathered. Davies feinted a lot in the middle rounds, trying to dummy his attacks and go to safer spaces in the ring. It wasn't enough to win rounds and his depleted energy levels were obvious. Gavin Rees was waiting to read the riot act in the corner and he did, asking Davies if he needed to throw the towel in. It was a rhetorical question, of course, and got the response required.

Davies reintroduced his jab in the eighth round and regained some form of control. It helped him to launch a huge assault, which started with a left cross and was followed by every other punch in the book, including the kitchen sink. Sadiq was forced to cover up and he lasted, even managing to respond before the round finished. It was Davies' last roll of the dice and he hadn't hit the jackpot.

"I haven't got the bottle to watch it back yet. It still hurts, so I haven't really tried yet. I didn't get hurt in the fight, I just didn't have no gas, and it's as simple as that. I didn't have no energy, nothing at all. I starved my body so much, I didn't have no reserves," offered Davies, explaining the unforeseen factors that dictated his largely dormant performance.

"Gavin was talking to me in the corner and we discussed a few things. I decided the best thing for me to do was ride it out for as long as possible and look for one big shot. I didn't have it in me to do anything else. That's what I tried, I landed the shot but I didn't have enough. I've learned a valuable lesson."

Sadiq's shots flicked away for the final two rounds, his quantity out-doing any quality Davies could muster the energy for. Davies looked resigned to defeat when the final bell rang, though Sadiq was an example of how to bounce back from a first professional loss. Sadiq was beaten the aforementioned Chelli in 2018.

The show was promoted by Frank Warren and featured several up-and-comers, live on BT Sport, to begin a big night of boxing. It served as an appetiser to Tyson Fury's destruction of Deontay Wilder for the WBC world title in Las Vegas. The heavyweight's troubles outside of the ring were well documented and Davies had faced his own personal tragedy. The reverberations from the unexpected and sudden loss of his older sister, Jade, a year ago were still being felt and it helped Davies to put his first professional loss into perspective.

He said: "I give all credit to Umar Sadiq, he did what he needed to do. Nevertheless, I think he was lucky to catch me on a day like that but it is what it is, I lost the fight and I'm going to move on. It gives me strength knowing that there's a lot more outside of boxing. All my life revolved around boxing so it was nice to realise boxing isn't everything."

All of Davies' post-fight analysis was delivered deadpan, a manner of self-assessment that's rarely found in boxing, a sport where reputations and perceived appearances are usually protected above all else. Egos can be fragile but Davies didn't hesitate to publicly point out his mistakes and unpick his flaws. He believed that mindset was the reason why he'll eventually succeed and achieve his goals.

"I'm real, that's what sets me apart from everyone else. No-one else is real anymore, especially in boxing. Everyone talks shit, plays the blame game and changes trainer after they lose. It is what it is. You win some, you lose some. It's not an attitude I've had before but it's an attitude I've had after my last fight.

"You realise what's important and what's not as important as you once thought. I'm just going to crack on, keep moving forward and hopefully get a good living and leave a legacy. That's all I can do."

Photo: Huw Fairclough

HARRIS EARNS HERO STATUS IN WORLD TITLE CHALLENGE
Saturday 29 February 2020

Boxers risk and sacrifice way too much to be happy with a loss on their record. The price they pay is made worthwhile by winning and receiving the rewards that come with it. However, Swansea's Jay Harris (17-1, 9KO) proved that there's an exception to the rule.

Aside from being bloodied and ultimately beaten, there was literally no reason for negativity when Harris left the ring after his first fight at world level. He travelled 4,750 miles from the Townhill district of his city to reach Frisco in Texas and had been given special leave from his part-time job as a forklift driver for online retailer Amazon. The appearance in the United States was nowhere near as low key as Harris' experiences in warehouses and the 29-year-old earned undoubted recognition as a world class boxer.

The official result was a unanimous decision win for Julio Cesar Martinez (16-1, 12KO), who retained his WBC world flyweight title after 12 brutal rounds that were packed with all the trouble the champion could handle. The scorecards read 118-109, 116-111 and 115-112 in favour of the Mexican, and the former was labelled as 'disgraceful' by Martinez's own promoter, Matchroom's Eddie Hearn. That scorecard was submitted by Herb Santos, a veteran of 750 fights that dated back to 1981, and it did no justice to Harris' efforts.

Although Harris accepted his status as an underdog, he was surprised at the pre-fight odds that saw him priced at 7/1. Those wide odds could have been forgiven as Martinez flew out of the traps. The 24-year-old's brute force made its mark in the opener. Harris' nose was bloodied and the rest of his face was reddened – it was a rough introduction to top level. Whilst Harris' was already distorted, Martinez's babylike features were deceiving and masked the bullish strength that made up for his technical deficiencies. It was the type of attack that stopped top talents like Barry's Andrew Selby, Charlie Edwards and Cristofer Rosales.

"I've said to everyone, the first round was probably my worst round. It was a pretty bad round for myself. I probably gave him too much respect," the Swansea City FC fan evaluated. "I do it all the time. I normally have a bad first round. I don't know why, it's just shit. I went back to the corner and had to compose myself.

"I knew about the odds because my friends and stuff were all taking bets on me. I was getting tagged in a lot of stuff on Instagram and Facebook. I knew what the odds were but I believed in my ability. I knew technically I was better than him but obviously he's strong and what have you. It didn't faze me. The bookies do get it wrong. They're not always correct."

Harris collected himself quickly and enjoyed his own moments in the second round. The Welshman was better technically, so he used his superior hand speed and fundamental skillset to score with straight shots, then followed it up with left hooks. Like any good champion, Martinez recognised the need to respond instantly and he rallied at the end of the third round, only to receive a flush right hand that Harris flung over the top like a frag grenade. The corner, headed by father Peter, a former British champion, were on high alert and called for more aggression to repel Martinez.

"What makes him pretty good is his unpredictability. As a boxer, when someone throws a right hand, you normally think a left hook or something like that is going to come over. In this case, he'd throw a right hand and on the same hand, he'd throw an uppercut or something mad," said Harris, astutely articulating the unorthodox danger. "It's quite hard to defend it. You just don't know what's going to come next. I think he throws what he feels. He doesn't really know what he's going to throw. That's what it feels like."

The distance shortened in the fourth round and they stood shoulder-to-shoulder for long spells. Harris picked up a small cut on his left eye and Martinez brutally targeted the body, as most Mexicans do. Martinez winged in punches from unusual angles in the fifth and sixth rounds. The shots, whether they landed or were blocked, sent thudding soundwaves around the ring. Harris wasn't far behind and clearly surprised the champion by staying with him, courtesy of a steady and accurate output.

Martinez began the seventh round with a serious onslaught and once the storm was weathered, it was Harris' time to respond. For all of Martinez's qualities, defence wasn't one of them and he was never hard to hit, so Harris stopped circling and obliged him. Another series of sharp straights backed Martinez up and led to further opportunities in the eighth round as Harris picked away at the gaping holes in defence.

"That's what we practiced in the gym a lot," revealed Harris, eager to stress that it was his pre-fight plan. "As soon as my back hit the ropes, get off. In his previous fights, as soon as he got them pinned down, he was a force and he blasted them apart. Our thing was if I ever touched the ropes, move away and get back to the centre again.

"I was the bigger fighter. Even though he was strong, there's a lot of parts in that fight when I took centre of the ring and I forced him back. If I'm being honest… if I got to fight him again, I'd probably do that a lot more often, try and push him back. He didn't like being on the back foot at all."

All of Harris' hard work was almost undone 18 seconds into the 10th round when two booming body shots bounced off either side of his rib cage. He'd stood too upright and invited attention to his torso. They were sickening blows and Harris was forced to take a knee, where he sucked up all of the oxygen available to recover and meet the count undertaken by referee Laurence Cole. Martinez had finally got through and he fancied his chances of closing the show.

Harris found himself in a worst-case scenario, especially late in the fight when tiredness becomes unavoidable. It would've been easier to stay down, after all he'd already proved the point that he can compete with world champions. But Harris is a fighter by blood and surrendering was never an option. Instead, Harris stood up and put on his best poker face amidst the increasing swelling around his eyes. He mustered all of his spirit into not only surviving the round but arguably winning it. The brilliant response, and threshold for pain, was unprecedented.

"What I can say… it wasn't so much of a knockout punch where he'd knock me clean out. It was more that every punch hurt. You could feel every punch pretty much and he loaded up with every punch he threw. Whatever he threw, he was trying to knock me out. I could take the power but it hurt," said Harris, unwilling to be the fall guy that others scripted.

"I could've taken the first body shot, the left one, but then he come through with the right and hit me on the opposite side. That took the wind out of me. I did the right thing and took the eight count. I thought if I stood up, it would've been much worse for me. I'd have probably got stopped. I got my breath back and when the referee said box on, I got on my bike for 30 seconds or so. I thought I've got to at least salvage a bit of the round and I thought I won the round after I got knocked down, I thought I did very well."

Harris cemented the effort of a lifetime in the championship rounds. The intensity had finally dropped, only slightly, and Harris worked away at distance. Martinez stuck to his clever tactics, upping his effort at the start and end of rounds, knowing he'd done enough to get a decision as the home fighter. Both embraced at the sound of the final bell, evidently oozing respect for each other after 36 manic minutes of fighting. The Mexican fans who booed, spat and threatened Harris during his ring walk, now stood and applauded his efforts in a signal of their respect for his performance.

"They were shouting stuff at me, spitting… it was disgusting. I was thinking 'what the hell have I come into?' I won the fans over in the end and got a great reception coming out," explained Harris, perplexed by the juxtaposition that partisan fans presented to him.

"It was kind of surreal. I've never really had it before. The messages of support I had off so many different people was unreal. Loads of Mexican people were saying how they're a fan of my style and how much of a warrior I am. That was the sort of compliments I got, 'warrior' and that stuff. It was a surreal moment for myself. I come out of the ring and pretty much got a standing ovation."

Gary Lockett, the manager who guided Harris to Commonwealth and European honours, bumped into an old foe during the build-up. The presence of Kelly Pavlik, the former world middleweight champion and last opponent of Lockett's career in 2008, indicated the status of the occasion. The show featured four-weight world champion Mikey Garcia, all-time great Roman Gonzalez and former heavyweight world champion Joseph Parker. At the end of it all, promoter Eddie Hearn singled out Harris' performance as the highlight of the night at the Ford Center, a training facility for the Dallas Cowboys - a prestigious American football team. DAZN and Sky Sports, the respective American and British broadcasters, also showered Harris with praise.

Mauricio Sulaiman, President of the WBC, was another Mexican hailing both boxers in the aftermath. He took to social media to say: "#MartinezHarris was an authentic war! Two warriors, who respect each other, giving their best in order to conquer greatness. Congratulations to both warriors!" Key decision makers in the sport were impressed and Harris was happy he'd seized his opportunity to make an impression.

He said: "I told everybody, 'I might not be here again so I'm going to fully embrace everything here.' The amount of people, the interviews... I took it all in my stride and embraced everything. It was fantastic to be a part of it. I'll never forget it. My first world title shot, one of the biggest cards to be put on and it wasn't even pay-per-view, people could watch it on Sky Sports. To be a part of that, such a great show and a big fight week, was fantastic."

The truth was that Harris may not have made history or left with the famous green and gold belt but he did improve all other aspects of his boxing life. The eyes of fans, broadcasters and promoters were opened. It undoubtedly enhanced his career and the prospect of financial security through boxing finally seemed realistic. Like many boxers, Harris had earned far less than minimum wage for all of the hours spent training in his seven years as a professional. He'd given serious consideration to walking away as recently as 18 months ago, only to be persuaded to persist by his father. The family was due to welcome a new daughter in the coming months and Harris could now harness boxing for its benefits, rather than be burdened by it.

"Hopefully, my performance will open more doors for me and better fights. Maybe we'll secure another world title shot by the end of the year or the start of next year. Pleasing the right people is a good thing. To work with Eddie Hearn would be unbelievable at this moment," smiled Harris, with a level of optimism that seemed unimaginable a short while ago.

"It's been worth it, let me tell you. Thanks to MTK [Global – promoter], they've come through with everything they've ever promised to me. We've only been together 18 months and I've had a world title shot in three fights.

"We're going to have a normal fight in the summer and we'll try to get another shot at a world title hopefully. That's what I'd love. I think I belong at this level, I certainly showed it."

Fittingly, Harris' leap of faith took place on a 'leap day.' Thankfully, he was almost certain to receive another big opportunity before the next 29 February. Back home in Swansea, it was already St David's Day by the time he flew the flag, representing his home city at world level like fellow natives Enzo Maccarinelli, Floyd Havard and Colin Jones did in their time.

Wales had a rich history in the flyweight division, too. Porth's Percy Jones became Wales' first world champion in 1914, soon to be followed by Tylorstown's Jimmy Wilde in 1916 and Cefn Fforest's Robbie Regan won the 'interim' IBF title in 1995. It was no longer unreasonable, or solely patriotic, to expect Harris to follow in their footsteps.

Photo: Liam Hartery

WHO DECLARE GLOBAL PANDEMIC BUT BOXING BEATS ON
Thursday 12 March 2020

The World Health Organisation [WHO] declared that the COVID-19 outbreak was a global pandemic as the scale of its deadly spread was realised.

After starting in China, cases of the highly infectious respiratory virus reached Europe with devastating consequences for public health. By this point, there were more than 20,000 confirmed cases in Europe and 1,000 deaths and the authorities were preparing for these numbers to skyrocket. Closer to home, there were nearly 600 cases confirmed in the UK and 10 people had died so far.

"More and more countries are now experiencing clusters of cases or community transmission," warned Dr Hans Henri P. Kluge, WHO Regional Director for Europe, in a public statement.

"We expect that in the days and weeks ahead, the number of cases and the number of deaths will continue to rise rapidly, and we must escalate our response in such a way as to take pre-emptive action wherever possible. Such actions may help to delay the pandemic, giving health-care systems time to prepare and assimilate the impact."

The BBBoC was widely regarded as one of the best governing bodies in the world. That wasn't to say the 91-year-old organisation was perfect, that's nearly impossible in a sport as subjective as boxing. License holders routinely questioned the selection of mandatory challengers for domestic titles, though that was usually done by disgruntled lobbyists. There was more legitimate criticism when it came to the BBBoC's senior officials and stewards, who were usually male and pale, and not exactly the most diverse group of decision makers. Boxers involved in criminal proceedings had, in the past, also felt unfairly treated by the BBBoC, especially when they hadn't been licensed to box if they were serving suspended sentences or out 'on license' after serving the custodial parts of their sentences. However, there were very few dissenting voices heard whenever the BBBoC's medical provisions were discussed. The BBBoC safety checks earned a stellar worldwide reputation.

Every BBBoC-licensed show mandated a significant medical presence. There must be at least two doctors present, including an anaesthetist, and they were often the first people into a ring when a fight ends to check both boxers before the result is announced. On the night, the doctors are supported by at least one ambulance and a team of paramedics, as well as a direct line to the neurosurgical unit of the nearest hospital in the event of a serious brain injury. Each of the BBBoC's seven 'areas' had a panel of doctors who meet to review regulations in between shows. The reason for the strict medical framework was to guarantee the highest standards of health and safety for boxers, as well as satisfying conditions of insurance cover.

The main reason why the COVID-19 pandemic was such a cause for concern for the BBBoC wasn't just their role to prevent mass gatherings and human-to-human transmission of viruses. If that was the biggest concern, it could be managed like it would be later down the line. Promoters with the backing of television broadcasters could carry on staging fights, they would just have to be held behind closed doors in sterile locations. Fans wouldn't be able to attend but, theoretically, there would be a captive audience watching at home to boost viewing figures.

However, that problem and its temporary solution was superseded by the simple fact that the National Health Service [NHS] fully expected to have no spare capacity when the COVID-19 pandemic grew in the UK from a few isolated clusters of cases to a full-blown outbreak. The healthcare service, set up by Tredegar-born Nye Bevan in 1948, was projecting an unprecedented strain and it needed all hands-on deck. Unsurprisingly, the doctors and paramedics who usually worked at boxing shows had much more important issues to prioritise over boxing, which was rightly put on the backburner along with every other non-essential activity.

Other combat sports like MMA felt the same effects, too. The UFC, the biggest promotional company in MMA, was due to hold its annual show in the UK on 21 March but they were forced to cancel their event at London's O2 Arena, which had sold out in a matter of hours. The knock-on effect saw Welsh fighters Jack Shore, Jack Marshman and John Phillips left in the lurch without a fight or a pay day.

Overall, the sporting world seemed to be sleepwalking to the COVID-19 problem for far too long. That was until the WHO's pandemic declaration, which triggered most major organisations to realise that urgent action was needed – the type of action that went far beyond hand sanitizer and social distancing. The noteworthy examples in the UK were football's Premier League and the Six Nations Rugby Championship, who both shelved plans for their multi-million-pound events. Perhaps enabled by its lack of overarching authority, boxing around the world typically bucked the trend and squeezed out one more weekend of fights.

There would be no COVID-19 protocols at the seven shows that took place in the UK over the weekend of 13-15 March 2020. They persisted with most attendees ignorant to the risk of virus transmissions spreading to athletes, coaches, officials, fans and their families.

THE ONLY SHOW IN TOWN
Saturday 14 March 2020

The COVID-19 pandemic wasn't the only challenge facing the joint Priority Boxing and MTK Global show at the Vale Sports Arena, which eventually went ahead as the only major sporting event in Cardiff that week.

Pontypool's Kieran Gething was originally due to headline against County Durham's dangerman Darren Surtees, only for a number of niggling injuries to end the Welsh super-lightweight champion's training camp. Then Cardiff's cruiserweight Nathan Thorley was set to meet Ireland's unbeaten Conor Cooke but interest, and ticket sales, drastically dropped when he was named as challenger for a Commonwealth title on Matchroom's show planned for 9 May. Lastly, featherweight Jacob Robinson (8-0) was matched with Spain's Carlos Ramos and COVID-19's widespread disruption to transport systems made it a hat-trick of cancellations. On top of that, cousins Fred Evans and Jamie 'JJ' Evans no longer featured on the undercard of what ended up being a six-fight show.

"Listen, I'm delighted that the show carried on. Y'know, we never really intended to pull it but we lost a lot of good quality fights. We were worried it wasn't going to be a good show but hopefully the fans enjoyed it," said Mo Prior, relieved to avoid a third straight cancellation after Priority Boxing's proposed Welsh shows in November and February fell through.

"This could be the last time they fight for a few months. These fighters have got to earn money and all that. Forget about the promoters, this could be the last time they fight for a few months. It gave the Welsh fans something good to watch because the rugby was cancelled and everything else was cancelled."

Robinson eventually faced Ukraine's Stanislav Bilohurov (0-2-1), out-pointing him over six uneventful rounds to prevail with a 60-54 decision. The 25-year-old clearly had the quality to score a knockout but he lacked the quantity to make it consistently uncomfortable for Bilohurov. The visitor was buzzed in the early rounds and unable to get to grips with Robinson's southpaw straights. The corner, headed by father Steve – former WBO world and European champion, beckoned Robinson forward. The requests were met with a surprising hesitancy. Perhaps underwhelmed by the change of opponent, Robinson allowed Bilohurov to duck and dodge his way around the ring until the final bell.

Cardiff's Maredudd Thomas (11-0, 2KO), who recently ended the apprenticeship phase of his career, was put on the backfoot for the first time as a professional against Sheffield-based Serge Ambomo (7-20-2, 3KO). The unbeaten welterweight was always the better boxer, earning a 60-54 decision win, and he showed a different side to his skillset over the course of six rounds. Opponents usually opted to evade Thomas' hard-hitting attacks but Ambomo, a 2012 Olympian for Cameroon, tried to do the opposite. 23-year-old Thomas varied the power and height of his shots and his patience pleased coach Gary Lockett. He was booked to travel to Bolton on 8 May to contest the WBC Youth title against hometowner Sahir Iqbal (7-0, 1KO).

Newport's Sean McGoldrick (10-1, 3KO) returned from his first professional defeat with a vengeance. He dished out four knockdowns to Stefan Slavchev (11-37-2, 4KO), one for every round that it took to get the fourth round stoppage win. The bantamweight missed out on the WBA Continental belt and a ranking when he slipped up against Cameroon's crafty Thomas Essomba in August, though showed no scars from the loss. McGoldrick, a two-time Commonwealth Games medallist, closed Slavchev's down with educated pressure. A short jab, smart footwork and targeted body shots took Slavchev's legs away and the tired Bulgarian frequented the floor. McGoldrick, under instruction from Jamie Moore, forced the finish by landing a series of chopping rights and referee Chris Jones had seen enough.

There was another fourth round stoppage for another Newport native as Craig Woodruff (10-5, 4KO) tore into the usually durable journeyman Joe Beeden (2-76-1, 1KO). Woodruff was as busy as a bee and the writing was on the fall after an intense start. The first knockdown came courtesy of Woodruff's uppercut, which sank deep into Beeden's stomach. The visitor rose too quickly and was sent down from a right to the side of his head moments later. 27-year-old Woodruff persisted and Beeden eventually succumbed to a flurry in the last round. It was just the sixth time Beeden had been stopped in 79 fights and it resulted in a mandatory 28 day medical suspension from the BBBoC.

It was unlikely the show would've gone ahead if it wasn't for Rhoose's Jay Munn (3-0). There was a strong show of support for the super-welterweight and his fans kept the show financially viable. In the ring, Munn was tasked with tracking down the ultra-unorthodox Victor Edagha (2-71-3, 1KO) and he succeeded with a 40-34 decision win over four rounds. Munn, trained by Chris Davies, applied a gradual pressure and it paid off in the third round when a booming right hand bounced Edagha into a neutral corner and then onto the floor. Munn kept a cool head but Edagha wanted to hold on to it, too. The problem was that the clinches Edagha initiated resulted in the loss of another point, deducted by referee Chris Jones in the last round. Promoter Eddie Hearn had been in contact before the fight and it was agreed that

Munn would appear on Matchroom's planned show in May, giving Munn's fans another reason to make noise.

Rhoose's lightweight Lance Cooksey (12-0, 2KO) was the eventual show-closer and he came through a tougher-than-expected six rounder with Birmingham's Daryl Pearce (1-11). The 29-year-old started with his typically busy two-fisted rallies but then grew more and more defensive. From the third round onwards, Cooksey's work was almost exclusively done with his left hand to suggest that his right hand may have been injured. It allowed Pearce into the fight and Cooksey, guided by Tony Borg, had to stay fleet footed to avoid trouble. Cooksey maintained his advantages in speed and progressed unbeaten. There were rumours of talks taking place for an all-Welsh showdown with Woodruff.

Five other shows took place across the UK on Saturday 14 March. Decision makers continued to make matches and plot paths for their boxers, blissfully unaware that the events they were planning wouldn't take place anytime soon.

Photos: Spencer Love & Liam Hartery

NORTH WALES TRIO STAY BUSY AND BUILD TOWARDS HOMECOMING
Saturday 14 March 2020

For a number of decades, it seemed like North Wales only had one professional boxer to represent the region at a time. Now there were three professionals and their activity was harnessing hopes that the north was building towards one of its most sustainable eras.

The trio – Gerome Warburton (6-0, 1KO), Sion Yaxley (6-0) and Osian Williams (2-0) – all trained under Wesley Jones at Dyffryn Boxing Club, a small gym in Colwyn Bay. The coach recognised the potential to create a new chapter of sporting history for North Wales and it was an inspiring thought behind their work.

"Starting off in the amateurs, we've done well, particularly for North Wales. We've had loads and loads of champions and the aim always was to get into the professional ranks," said Jones, believing their success would have a knock-on effect for the next generation. "We've got some outstanding youngsters in the club already. They look up to these lads. That's the key. Everyone from the bottom up want to be like them. That's what the aim is and it [success] will snowball."

All three prospects were busy in recent times and it continued with a triplet of wins at the Bolton Whites Hotel, in a function room attached to the Macron Stadium, home of Bolton Wanderers FC.

Colwyn Bay's Gerome Warburton lived a matter of miles away from Dyffryn Boxing Club and the craftily nicknamed 'Bread Maker' had trained with Jones since his early teenage years. They enjoyed 60 fights together in the amateurs, making Warburton the most experienced boxer in the gym. The 24-year-old's sixth professional fight was a straightforward four round affair. Warburton, a super-welterweight southpaw, outworked veteran journeyman Kevin McCauley (15-207-12), who was rarely stopped and an expert in suffering Britain's best up-and-comers.

"I was very happy with his [Warburton's] performance," summarised Jones. "Kevin McCauley is very experienced, well over 200 professional fights. Gerome handled him very easily. He tried to get the stoppage one point, it didn't quite happen. He's very battled hardened is Kevin McCauley.

"I would say, he needs to push on now and try get a bit more competitive [fights]. Although you do learn with the likes of Kevin McCauley, they generally come to mess you around and make you look bad. Gerome still looked good but he needs a bit of a test next, I think."

Referee Andy Brook had the easy task of filing a 40-36 scorecard and Bristol-based management Sanigar Events were tasked to find more threatening opponents. Warburton had already proven he was capable of facing adversity, too. He found himself in the away corner on his debut in early 2019 and he ran over fellow debutant Celal Ozturk in two rounds at London's York Hall. Jones believed the well-supported Ozturk took Warburton lightly and they remained ready to upset anyone else who would overlook them.

Ruthin's Sion Yaxley was the longest serving boxer at Dyffryn Boxing Club. He progressed with a routine 40-36 decision win over Danny Little (8-68-2, 1KO), the second time the two boxers had fought each other. Like all of Yaxley's professional bouts, he was a class above. Routine wins like that can help new professionals acclimatise to the intangible elements of their new surroundings, like the atmosphere and occasion, but there was little left for Yaxley to learn in fights of that type.

Like Warburton, Yaxley also competed at super-welterweight and he hoped his management, again Sanigar Events, would produce matches to really test his talents. Both boxers eyed a shot at the Welsh title in the near future and Jones was hopeful a bout could be arranged with champion Tony Dixon. For Yaxley, the 23-year-old had a quality 50-fight amateur career that included a senior Welsh title win and repeating the feat as a professional was a high priority.

Observing the scene, Jones said: "There's some decent boxers at Welsh title level. The obvious one in and around Sion and Gerome's weight is Tony Dixon but I'd be quite happy with either going up to that sort of calibre of opponent at the moment. I'd be pretty confident they'd win or, if not, do very well and push it very close.

"With Gerome, he's had a lot of amateur fights. Win or lose, he just wants to box all the time, he's one of them types. He definitely needs to push on, more so with Gerome than Sion at this moment. It's just because Sion's got a lot of tools in the bag and he's progressing really well, there's no mad rush but with Gerome, he's a bit bored with run of the mill contests."

It was earlier days for 29-year-old Osian Williams, the gym's most recent addition. The welterweight was born in St Asaph and later moved across the border, training in Salford under the highly respected Oliver Harrison, who passed away from cancer in April 2019. The Manchester connection saw Williams recruited as a sparring partner for former WBA world champion Anthony Crolla and that experience made his mind up to turn professional. A move to Conwy coincided with the decision and Williams, nicknamed 'The Hurricane', joined Jones at Dyffryn Boxing Club after a stint on the unlicensed circuit.

Williams debuted in January and had a quick turnaround for his second professional outing, coming through a trickier-than-expected four rounder with Qasim Hussain (4-104-2). Referee Andy Brook scored it 39-37 to Williams, who pledged to move down in weight for his future fights. Williams was managed directly by Kieran Farrell and eager to take whatever dates came his way.

"He's very, very dedicated. He's a good addition. The three of them are all very dedicated but Osian's whole life is boxing, everything. He's never out of shape, he's always on his diet, he's very good," said Jones, before beginning his explanation of why there were lessons to be learned from 'run of the mill' fights for the likes of Williams.

"It was a very tricky opponent, who I hadn't seen previously. He tried to wind Osian up, pulling his head down and a lot of dirty tricks. In one round, Osian fell for the tricks and got a bit too involved. We had to calm him down and he went back to his boxing. It was pretty comfortable in the end. They're not trying to win, they're trying to make you look bad. Like I say, he did make Osian look particularly bad in one round. It's just a case of sticking to your boxing and not allowing them. They're teaching you things, getting you frustrated and you've got to learn to keep your cool. It's very important."

The show was promoted by Kieran Farrell, one of the busiest promoters in the whole of Britain. Farrell's own career in the ring ended when he suffered a brain injury in an English title challenge against Crolla. The lightweight was only 22-years-old when tragedy struck and he had since made a remarkable recovery. Farrell established his promotional company in 2016 and the North West of England's close proximity to North Wales helped to keep Warburton, Yaxley and Williams active.

"It's been a godsend for us, to be honest. The obvious thing is, most of Chris' [Sanigar] boxers are in South Wales and in Bristol. From North Wales, it's as far away as you can get, boxing-wise. We've got in with Kieran Farrell and the good thing is Sion and Gerome both sell a lot of tickets. I mean, they're selling 70 tickets each time which easily covers the opponent, wages for themselves and money for the promoter," said Jones, optimistic that it would build towards fight nights on the Welsh side of the northern border.

"We've spoken with Chris and he's expressed an interest [in promoting a show in North Wales] if we can find the right venue. He's good to go. We need probably five contests. We've got three in our stable and it's a case of finding another couple of boxers in North Wales. I'm sure between Sion, Gerome and Osian, they can sell 500 tickets plus. That's a good start, isn't it?"

A homecoming wasn't a necessity for the moment but it was out there, on the horizon for North Wales. "Giving our lads a good chance," was Jones' eternal incentive.

OUT, INJURED, POSTPONED: OLYMPIC QUALIFICATION AVOIDS WELSH TRIO

PART I
Sunday 15 March 2020

There's a fine line between success and failure for international amateur boxers at the highest level and it can depend on the luck of the draw, or lack of luck in the case of Caldicot's Rosie Eccles.

Aside from those who receive a seeded position, tournaments draws are a lottery and don't discriminate against anyone from anywhere. It can have a huge influence on the outcome of a tournament, enhancing the chances of a medal for some and reducing it for others. All participating boxers accept the ruthless reality of their situation in a refreshing contrast to their more selective counterparts in the professional code.

Over 300 boxers travelled to London, despite the COVID-19 pandemic, to fight for 77 places at the 2020 Olympics in Tokyo, Japan. The qualifier was named 'The Road to Tokyo' and it was the first chance for European boxers to qualify with 50 places on offer to the men and 27 to the women.

Eccles, 23, received a bye in the first round of the qualifier and so did Russia's Sadaat Dalgatova. The welterweights met in the second round and there was hardly anything between them. The judges did manage to decide a winner and they favoured Dalgatova, who was awarded narrow split decision win to damage Eccles' Olympic dream.

Keen to use her size advantage, Eccles poured the pressure on in the first round. Dalgatova, a bronze medallist at the recent World Championships, spun to the sides and countered often enough to earn the session with three of the five judges. It gave the Russian a strong foothold in the fight and Eccles couldn't afford to let another round pass her by.

Eccles was able to enjoy more success in the second round when she doubled down on her physical tactics. Dalgatova found it difficult to avoid constant waves of attack and often resorted to clinches to catch a break, dipping low before rising back up in a messy tangle of limbs. Four of the five judges appreciated Eccles' efforts to level the scorecards and the fight was sent down to the wire.

The action didn't get much cleaner in the third round and it concluded a missed opportunity for Eccles. The sneaky skills of Dalgatova meant she was able smother most of the replies coming her way before the referee broke them up. Three of the five judges edged it to Dalgatova again and Eccles was eliminated from the qualifier.

There was a sparse crowd at the Copper Box Arena. The poor showing was undoubtedly impacted by COVID-19. The event was arguably the best value for money boxing fans had seen on British shores for a long time. Tickets were priced at £5 and some of the world's best talents were scheduled to perform. The underwhelming atmosphere was a complete contrast to the scene in 2012 when the same venue was packed out with thousands of fans, who cheered Team GB onto three Olympic gold medals.

By the end of the evening session, the IOC's BTF decided that an even smaller group of people would get to see the boxing in person. The remainder of the qualifier, it was announced, would take place behind closed doors as further measures were taken to stop the spread of COVID-19.

PART II
Monday 16 March 2020

After dropping down from light-heavyweight, Swansea's Sammy Lee was set to compete at middleweight. However, a shoulder injury ruled the Commonwealth Games gold medallist out three weeks before the qualifier.

The Welshman was replaced by Colchester's Lewis Richardson. The 22-year-old substitute began his campaign against France's Victor Yoka and his work from the southpaw stance was impressive. Richardson manoeuvred his way to a unanimous decision win and he needed just two more wins to secure his spot at the Olympics.

Unlike other Olympic cycles, Team GB made a decision not to allow more than one boxer per weight category to qualify. The selectors previously allowed it to happen, in the rare occasions it was possible, and ordered "box-offs" between the two qualified boxers to determine who proceeded to the Olympics. Andrew Selby and Kal Yafai was a classic example of the policy in 2012. The change meant that if Richardson qualified, Lee wouldn't be sent to the next Olympic qualifier, which was scheduled for Paris, France. It was effectively a first come first served policy.

Later that day, UK Prime Minister Boris Johnson held the first of his daily press conferences to update the country on England's response to COVID-19. Flanked by the Chief Medical Adviser and Chief Scientific Adviser for the UK Government, Johnson briefed viewers of the measures being taken to delay the spread of the disease. The repercussions for boxing, and all mass gatherings, were inevitable.

"It remains true, as we said in the last few weeks, that the sort of transmissions of the disease at mass gatherings, such as sporting events, are relatively low," began Johnson, treading a familiar tightrope that prompts some people to regard him as a world class waffler, whilst his supporters perceive his elongated delivery of key messages to be a perfectly appropriate method of communication in a time of worldwide crisis.

"But obviously, logically, as we advise against unnecessary social contact of all kinds, it's right that we should extend that advice to mass gatherings as well.

"And so we've also got to ensure that we have the critical workers we need that might otherwise be deployed for those gatherings, to deal with these emergencies. So from tomorrow, we will no longer be supporting mass gatherings with emergency workers in the way that we normally do."

The Welsh Government, who were responsible for health under the devolution of statutory powers, followed suit immediately and it was now official: medical professionals had a much bigger priorities, so sport and boxing were put on pause.

PART III
Tuesday 17 March 2020

On the fourth day of 'The Road to Tokyo,' news filtered through that the morning session wouldn't begin and the Olympic qualifier would end nine days early.

The IOC BTF took the decision to postpone the event in light of the COVID-19 related measures being rolled out across the country and continent. The safeguarding of participants and officials was the IOC BTF's main concern and it made the decision "to allow the participants from over 60 countries to adjust their travel plans and return home."

Up until this point, only 16 boxers had qualified for the 2020 Olympics. It left 61 places for the remaining 168 boxers and that unqualified pool of boxers included Ystrad Mynach's Lauren Price. The reigning world middleweight champion was drawn to face France's rangy Davina Michel in the afternoon session but they would have to wait. The IOC BTF promised that the qualifier would restart where it left off when it was safe, but nobody could have any confidence when that would be.

Boris Johnson was back in another press conference by late afternoon and he described the public health measures being taken to stop the spread of COVID-19 as "steps that are unprecedented since World War Two." It was an ominous statement for amateur boxers given that World War Two was the cause of the last cancelled Olympic Games.

COVID-19 LOCKDOWN CANCELS THE CALENDAR

PART I
Monday 23 March 2020

Once confirmation came that COVID-19 was to halt boxing for the foreseeable future, it came quickly and coincided with an unprecedented nationwide 'lockdown.'

It began on Monday 23 March when the BBBoC issued a statement at midday to suspend all professional shows under their jurisdiction. The statement outlined their undeniable logic and their intention to review the situation at the end of April. That was a silver lining, of sorts, but even the most eternal of optimists understood the pandemic was unlikely to be resolved by then.

Later in the evening, the UK Government announced a number of 'lockdown' restrictions, the most significant in modern memory, in an attempt to slow the spread of COVID-19. The police were given powers to make sure people stayed at home, only leaving to shop for necessities, for limited exercise or to travel to essential work. Similar measures were also implemented by the Welsh Government.

COVID-19 had caused 335 deaths and there were 6,650 confirmed cases of the infection in the UK at this point. Public health experts predicted the UK was two weeks behind Italy and expected to follow a similar trajectory. Italy was devastated, with over 10,800 deaths and 98,000 confirmed cases. Ominously, the number of Italian cases were still rising and showed no signs of slowing anytime soon.

The BBBoC announcement caused widespread disruption to the Welsh boxing calendar. Postponements were promptly announced for; Morgan Jones' vacant Welsh middleweight title fight with Geraint Goodridge on 28 March in Swansea, Chris Jenkins' British and Commonwealth welterweight title rematch with Johnny Garton on 11 April in London, and Craig Evans' 25 April trip to Belfast to face rising star Sean McComb. Several agreed fights that were yet to be announced were also affected.

PART II
Tuesday 24 March 2020

The next day was the turn of amateur boxing's authorities. The IOC and the Tokyo 2020 Organising Committee made a joint announcement: "In the present circumstances and based on the information provided by the WHO today, the IOC President and the Prime Minister of Japan have concluded that the Games of the XXXII Olympiad in Tokyo must be rescheduled to a date beyond 2020 but not later than summer 2021, to safeguard the health of the athletes, everybody involved in the Olympic Games and the international community.

"The leaders agreed that the Olympic Games in Tokyo could stand as a beacon of hope to the world during these troubled times and that the Olympic flame could become the light at the end of the tunnel in which the world finds itself at present. Therefore, it was agreed that the Olympic flame will stay in Japan. It was also agreed that the Games will keep the name Olympic and Paralympic Games Tokyo 2020."

Their decision to postpone the Olympic and Paralympic Games for a year, on a yet-to-be specified date in 2021, was enormously important. There were only three other times in recent history when the Olympics hadn't taken place on schedule. The Olympics were cancelled in 1940 and 1944 as Nazi Germany waged war on the world and the 1972 event was suspended for 34 hours when Palestinian terrorists killed 11 Israeli athletes and a police officer in Munich, then-West Germany.

Nonetheless, the IOC's position was decisive. It meant that Ystrad Mynach's Lauren Price, Caldicot's Rosie Eccles and Swansea's Sammy Lee, along with hundreds of other athletes, would have to wait at least another year to realise their dreams in Tokyo. Two weeks ago, the dream of a lifetime, a chance to medal at the Olympics, was just four months away and the years of visualisation were about to become reality. The new reality was a rapidly developing situation. Team GB, had to carefully adapt their support structures and replan. Precautions would be needed to make sure the boxers, who were funded by the National Lottery, avoided going stale or struggled to stay at the weight for another year.

COVID-19 was also an issue for amateur boxing clubs in Wales. Welsh Boxing, the organisation who govern amateur boxing in the country, postponed the Welsh Championships for all age categories from April to an unannounced date later in 2020.

The decision to postpone the Olympics to 2021 showed there were lessons learned from the recently postponed Olympic qualifier in London, which attracted criticism for hesitantly handling the situation. The IOC's BTF initially decided to reduce the crowds on day three of the event by holding it behind closed doors, only to backtrack a day later and postpone it altogether. In the aftermath, six members of participating boxing teams tested positive for COVID-19 when they returned home. The Turkish Boxing Federation were the most vocal critics, blaming the delayed decision-making for the infections contracted by two of their boxers and a coach.

Blaenavon's former boxer Mason Jones was the only Welshman who managed to fight around this time. The 24-year-old left the squared circle in 2017, walking away from a 3-0 record as a promising prospect in professional boxing to pursue another career in combat. Jones embarked on the octagons of MMA and thrived under the banner of Cage Warriors, a European-based promotional company and an established feeder route to the domineering UFC. Cage Warriors, led by Irishman Graham Boylan, refused to relent to pressure and found a way to hold their show on 20 March amidst the COVID-19 pandemic, just days before the government announced their full restrictions. Headlining an empty arena in Manchester was an odd setting, though didn't deter Jones from hammering Joe McClogan for a first-round finish to capture the Cage Warriors lightweight world title.

PART III
Monday 30 March 2020

A lot can happen in a week. The number of deaths in the UK rose to 1,408 on Monday 30 March and the number of confirmed cases was now at 19,522. The true number was likely to be far higher. The BBBoC's General Secretary Robert Smith extended the suspension of professional boxing for the month of May and promised to "keep the situation under review and when possible explore all options available to find a way of lifting the suspension when conditions permit."

That forced the hand of Eddie Hearn's Matchroom. Three weeks earlier, the promoter held a press conference at the plush Exchange Hotel in Cardiff to announce a big night of boxing at the Motorpoint Arena. It would've been the first time Matchroom visited the venue in six years but it seemed a distant memory as the country closed down.

Barry's Lee Selby was set to face Australia's George Kambosos Jr in a final eliminator for the IBF world lightweight title, Cardiff's Joe Cordina was being lined up to face a former world champion at super-featherweight, Trelewis' Gavin Gwynne would get a second shot at the British lightweight title, plus Nathan Thorley was due to challenge for the Commonwealth title at cruiserweight. As far as shows in Wales go, it didn't get much bigger but none of it would happen on Saturday 9 May as previously planned. A caveat was offered by Matchroom, stating the show would instead go ahead on Saturday 11 July and that was very ambitious. Even if it had been achievable, it would've required boxers to compete after barely being able to prepare properly because gyms were subject to the shutdown restrictions.

Everything was on lockdown. Whenever the full scale seemed to be realised, another unprecedented step was taken. Boxing, and sport in general, remained firmly at the back of authorities' priorities. That fact was demonstrated when the NHS set up field hospitals at Llanelli's Parc y Scarlets stadium and Cardiff's Principality Stadium.

MOHAMMED HASHIM JEÉRACKS MOURNED AFTER TRAGIC DEATH
Tuesday 7 April 2020

Waking up to the tragic news that Cardiff's promising talent Mohammed Hashim Jeéracks had died, at just 18-years-old, hurt the Welsh boxing community.

In the early hours of Tuesday 7 April, at around 1:30am, a serious road traffic accident happened between junction 14 and 15 of the M4, near Membury Services in Swindon. Jeéracks was in a BMW car that hit the central reservation of the motorway and he died as a result of the collision. A 19-year-old female passenger, who remained unnamed, suffered minor injuries, too.

Jeéracks was schooled by Carl Stephens, head coach of Llanedeyrn Boxing Club, and won 31 of his 36 amateur fights. His achievements included Welsh and British Championship wins, and he represented his country numerous times. He decided to turn professional in July 2019 and signed a managerial contract with Gary Lockett. Sparring sessions with hardened professionals like Jay Harris and Andrew Selby ensued and talk of special performances in the gym soon spread. Known as 'Little Mo' or 'Baby Mo' in the gym, he was said to be a match for his senior stablemates.

"He had recently been training with accomplished professionals such as Andrew Selby and Jay Harris, who had recently boxed for world titles," stated Carl Stephens, who coached Jeéracks since he was 10-years-old.

"Mo was just a young man compared to these seasoned boxers but they could not believe the ability he had with his limited experience. There were a lot of well-placed people on the boxing circuit who thought Little Mo could have gone right to the top.

"Mo was like second son to me. He was a likeable, bubbly, smiling young man who everyone loved. It is a tragedy for his family, friends and all the boxing world that such a talent has been lost at such a young age.

"The boys at the gym will carry on in your memory and do their best to box in your shadow. Little Mo - simply the best."

The Jeéracks family launched a fundraiser and they set an ambitious goal of £18,000. It was collected in a matter of weeks as more than 1,100 individual donations were made. The money was to be used to fund seven wells around the world in Mo's name. Built by the Muslim Hands charity, the wells would help people in Gambia, Mali, Niger, Pakistan, Senegal, Somalia and Sudan. Leftover money was given to Wan Aid, a smaller charity that organised school meals for poor children in Sudan.

OMAR OPTS FOR NEW PATH AS PROFESSIONAL PRIZEFIGHTER
Wednesday 29 April 2020

Three years on from a life-threatening stabbing, Cardiff's Rashid Omar decided to add another chapter to his eventful story and embark on a new journey as a professional prizefighter.

Omar won schoolboy and youth Welsh titles as an amateur, earning the nickname of 'Brickfists' from his supporters. His vested career started with the Prince of Wales ABC and he owed the success as a senior to training at Splott Adventure ABC. Omar's path was derailed in July 2017 when he suffered a scary setback as the victim of a serious attack. Three knife wounds, including one that punctured 5cm into his liver, resulted in a year out of the ring.

"I was on a night out and I got into a little argument," he recalled. "There was an altercation and the guy stabbed me three times. It stopped me from training for a year. All the nurses and doctors said it might stop me from boxing permanently.

"It was hard. When I first come out of hospital, I couldn't even walk the stairs without using an asthma pump. It was really hard fitness-wise. I was devastated but it made me more determined, it made me stronger. I had to get myself better."

Omar acknowledged that he was lucky to survive the attack and avoid becoming yet another statistic of a growing knife crime problem in the UK. In the immediate aftermath, the father of four was supported by amateur trainers Pat Mahoney and James Mwasigallah and he committed to an extensive rehabilitation programme. Omar began plotting a path to the Olympics and decided to target the upcoming qualifying events, attending through his Somali heritage.

Somalia's relationship with boxing had seen its fair share of turbulence over the past five decades. Dictator Mohamed Siyad Barre issued a ban on boxing in 1976 and all sports were suspended when Somalia descended into a chaotic civil war in 1991. The country was considered a 'failed state' in the following years due to the absence of a centralised government and the uncertainty was cemented when United Nations peacekeepers withdrew later in the 1990s. It meant Somali sportspeople had to leave the country to compete on the international stage as independent athletes.

The Federal Government formed in 2012 and it helped Somalia to slowly edge towards stability. The first boxing events for decades were held in 2018. Boxing's return to Somalia coincided with the appointment of Hassan Essa to Technical Development Director for the Somali Boxing Federation, the country's national governing body for amateurs. Cardiff-born Essa won a Welsh amateur title in 1997 and then fulfilled various roles for Grange Catholics ABC in Grangetown. Known to Omar's parents, Essa's input was crucial and he invited the southpaw to trials in London.

Omar was selected and he travelled to Gabon, on the west coast of central Africa, to compete in the African Championships in May 2019. The highlight performance was a win against Namibia's Jonas Jonas, who won a gold medal at the 2018 Commonwealth Games, and Omar progressed all the way to the final. He eventually lost to Cameroon's Mengue Ayissi but a silver medal at a major tournament was still a significant achievement. Now qualification to the 2020 Olympics was firmly on the agenda. However, the podium appearance in Gabon would prove to be the last of Omar's 70-fight amateur career.

He said: "They [his family] were very proud and the whole community was. In Butetown, it's predominantly a Somali community. Everyone was stopping me in the street, especially the older generation who never thought it [a Somalian a boxing team] would happen.

"It was amazing but the Somali team ain't got much funding. They wanted me to fund myself to go to all of these tournaments. I didn't really think that was good."

Contact was established with Tom Stalker, who captained Team GB at the 2012 Olympics and now worked for management outfit MTK Global as their Chief Scout. The Scouser was impressed with the video clips he saw and they quickly came to an agreement for Omar to turn professional. Tony Borg took the role of Omar's trainer and the transition also included a drop of 11 pounds. He shed the surplus weight and came down from super-lightweight (141lbs) to compete as a super-featherweight (130lbs) in the pro-code.

Training during the COVID-19 pandemic was obviously disrupted. 'Lockdown' restrictions set by the Welsh Government meant everyone, sportsperson or not, was subject to limited exercise and what was allowed had to be in their immediate locality. Omar enjoyed running and cycling around Cardiff Bay, however there was no substitute for punching and he was eager to return to Borg's St Joseph's Boxing Club in Newport.

"I've been training in there for the last seven months," said Omar. "I've learned loads up there. I've got great sparring with the likes of Lee Selby, Gavin Gwynne, Lance Cooksey and Robbie Vernon. We're all around the same weight, so we're all learning from each other.

"All of my training [since lockdown] has been limited. I've been doing pads in my garden a couple of times a week but I've been doing plenty of bike riding and running, every day."

Prior to the pandemic, Omar hoped to turn professional on the undercard of Eddie Hearn's postponed Matchroom show in Cardiff on 9 May. He was uncertain when he'd be able to make his debut but was certain of what he wants to do when boxing returns.

"I definitely want to be fast tracked. I wouldn't mind having, say, two or three type of easy fights to get used to the pro ranks but I don't want to be waiting around. I want to be fighting for titles straight away.

"I want to fight for the Welsh title but my goal is more than that. I want to fight for British and European titles, and possibly a world title."

SELBY'S WORLD TITLE ELIMINATOR SUCCUMBS TO COVID-19, AGAIN

Wednesday 3 June 2020

Eddie Hearn's Matchroom finally submitted to the reality of the COVID-19 pandemic and rescheduled Lee Selby's (28-2, 9KO) IBF world title eliminator. A third, and hopefully final, date was announced for one of the most important fights of Selby's career.

It became obvious that COVID-19 wouldn't disappear before the meeting with George Kambosos Jnr (18-0, 10KO) at Cardiff's Motorpoint Arena and it forced Hearn's reluctant hand. Government rules at the time of the announcement also meant the power-punching lightweight would've been required to self-isolate for two weeks after his arrival from Australia, which wasn't deemed practical.

The duo were first set to fight on 9 May, which was then moved to 11 July and finally reset to 3 October. It meant a delay of at least five months and the situation would exhaust the patience of many boxers. Added to that, Selby admitted uncertainty that mass-gatherings would even be allowed in the autumn. His management, Sanigar Events, couldn't exactly receive assurances from the relevant authorities and fighting behind closed doors may become their only option.

"If they reschedule it, I'll get on with it," he said. "I think it will take place on that date [3 October] but I'm not sure whether there will be fans. There are fights going to take place behind closed doors and I wouldn't be surprised if mine was the same.

"It is what it is. I see it how it is, my fight is nothing compared to what's going on. Everybody is going through the same thing. I'm nothing special, so I'll get on with it.

"When we were asked if we were okay to box behind closed doors, I said 'yes' straight away. It's just a fight at the end of the day. My best performances haven't been in the ring in front of fans, it's been in the gym with no-one there. I've sparred all over the world, I've sparred in America against top class fighters and I barely lose a round."

The disruption to the boxing calendar, which completely stagnated for three months, was easily put into perspective. On the day Matchroom announced the rearranged date for Selby's fight, the UK had recorded a total of 154,729 cases of COVID-19 and 39,728 related deaths. They were sobering statistics.

There were no government furlough payments to supplement fight purses that went unearned. Boxers sat on the sidelines without financial support or guaranteed safety nets. Most notably in Wales, Clydach's middleweight Liam Williams was awaiting a challenge to WBO world champion Demetrius Andrade and Cardiff's super-featherweight Joe Cordina was being lined up to face Puerto Rico's former world champion Roman Martinez. However, both of those fights were yet to be confirmed, whereas Selby's fight was signed, sealed and on sale.

In years gone by, Selby regularly visited the gyms of Los Angeles and Las Vegas to sharpen his skills in the harshest of training environments. Those trips had sometimes doubled up as scouting missions and helped him to get a look at other hungry contenders who share the same ambitions. Sparring partners had even become opponents, most notably Australian Joel Brunker who was defeated for the first time in nine rounds of a final eliminator for the IBF featherweight title in 2014.

Like his countryman, Kambosos Jr had also sparred Selby in America and they both gained an insight to the other's abilities in 2018. Selby was satisfied that he took away an informed opinion of Kambosos Jr, though wasn't sure the Aussie's assessment was as accurate. The closest they'd come to being reacquainted was an e-press conference, where a confident Kambosos Jr predicted an easy win and the end of Selby's career. The statement, delivered in the forthright fashion typical of an assured unbeaten boxer, crossed the line in the eyes of everyone except Selby.

"It's water off a duck's back. Every fighter has a load to say," shrugged Selby. "I watched him spar four rounds before he sparred me, against a Scottish boy [Nathaniel Collins] who was an amateur at the time and he looked good.

"The Scottish kid was a southpaw and Kambosos throws a lovely right uppercut and he kept catching him with the uppercut and bloodied his nose. When I got in there, I upped my game but it was just like normal sparring. He didn't seem like nothing special. Watching him, he looks very fast but when I was in there, he didn't seem very fast.

"When we did this e-press conference, Kambosos said he had me running all around the Wildcard [gym] and shook me to my boots every time he hit me. That's given me some confidence because I know it didn't happen. If he believes that, he's bloody deluded."

Selby usually enlisted the skills of Trelewis' Gavin Gwynne as a sparring partner. The gym-mates had shared hundreds of rounds together at St Joseph's Boxing Club in Newport. Their latest collaboration, away from trainer Tony Borg, was slightly different with Gwynne's hands instead put to use as a tradesman. The Welsh lightweight champion converted Selby's garage into a home gym, equipped with all of the kit he needed to stay relatively active during lockdown. It was a useful workaround when the Welsh Government limited travel for exercise to a five mile radius.

Gwynne was preparing to fight for the British lightweight title against Belfast's banger James Tennyson in August. It would take place at Eddie Hearn's Fight Camp, a series of shows situated in the back garden of the Matchroom mansion in Essex to comply with COVID-19 restrictions. The financial limits of the shows meant it wasn't viable for Selby vs Kambosos Jr, so he'd have to make do with his garage workouts for now.

Selby said: "Gavin Gwynne has come down and turned my double garage into a lovely boxing gym, it's a top of the range boxing gym. I've got all the Everlast bags, I've got six bags, I've got a multi-weight gym, a cross trainer and I did have a treadmill but it's just packed in. I've run it into the ground.

"It was something I never wanted in my house, a gym. I'm always in the gym and always training, so when you come home, that's your place to chill but with this pandemic, I've had no choice."

Away from boxing, Selby was kept on his toes during lockdown. Parenthood couldn't be put on pause and, along with his partner, the 33-year-old was busy delivering home schooling to his three children. Teaching an adapted curriculum and maintaining the upkeep of a mini-farm yard, that accommodated nearly 40 animals, provided a substitute focus and made daily routines less monotonous.

Thoughts of regaining another world title and making Welsh history as an official two-weight world champion were never far away from his mind, though. Vasili Lomachenko, arguably already an all-time great, reigned at the top of the lightweight division. The Ukrainian's legendary amateur career included a win over younger brother Andrew Selby and culminated in a second Olympic gold medal in 2012. He continued to set records after turning professional and won world titles in three weight categories. By his 15th fight, Lomachenko owned the WBA, WBO and WBC belts at lightweight. In an indictment of boxing's broken multi-belt system, the WBC then 'upgraded' Lomachenko to the newly invented position of 'franchise' champion and confused everyone. It was a cynical decision, taken to allow American Devin Haney to have an undoubtedly watered-down version of the WBC's championship without having to risk losing to Lomachenko.

Still, Lomachenko was recognised as the leader at lightweight and he was being lined up with Teofimo Lopez, an exciting rising star from New York who held the IBF belt – the missing piece. Both Lomachenko and Lopez were promoted by Bob Arum's Top Rank and a meeting seemed inevitable when boxing resumed. It was common knowledge that whoever became the undisputed champion was likely to change weight divisions, but in opposite directions. Lomachenko was expected to go down to super-featherweight, nearer his natural size, and Lopez upwards to embrace his maturing physical frame.

Selby recognised that he may be left to fight for a vacant title but still harboured hopes of dethroning a reigning champion, especially one with the prestige of Lomachenko. The path of least resistance was, conversely, so often trodden in boxing. Risk-averse handlers, who are plentiful in boxing, would advise Selby against opting for Lomachenko when a vacant title shot against the next ranked challenger would likely be easier. Unsurprisingly, it wasn't a school of thought a throwback fighter like Selby willingly subscribed to and he was conflicted about the best scenario.

"If I beat Kambosos, I could end up fighting for the vacant title," he contemplated carefully. "There's two ways to look at it. You could either have a mega payday or a much better chance of winning a world title and to me, I'd rather win the world title.

"Facing the winner of that [Lomachenko vs Lopez] is a massive fight, a life changing fight financially. Anything can happen in boxing, so you can't write me off, even though I'd be a big underdog.

"I'd be the first Welshman to be a two-weight world champion. It's massive, it's better than any money in the ring. It's making history."

Photo: Liam Hartery

PROJECT RESTART: BUSINESS AS UNUSUAL
Friday 10 July 2020

Starting boxing's recovery from the COVID-19 pandemic was an unparalleled challenge, on both a national and international scale.

The economic downturn had an inevitable impact on the majority of people in boxing. The few boxers who earn multimillion-pound purses could withstand the inactivity because they usually fought twice a year. However, those further down the food chain were put under serious stress. There were more than 1,100 professional boxers in the UK and whatever a 'new normal' would look like, there was increased uncertainty for everyone.

Welsh Boxing, the national governing body for amateur boxing in Wales, were constantly kept busy as they worked to keep volunteer-led amateur clubs in Wales alive and informed. They crucially signposted to lifelines from Sport Wales, such as the Emergency Relief Fund. The fund gave immediate financial support to 23 not-for-profit boxing clubs, who were part of a group of nearly 400 sports clubs to receive a collective £600,000. When the fund closed, the Be Active Wales Fund was launched to protect and prepare Welsh sport to survive the pandemic. It distributed £4m and individual clubs were able to apply for grants of £300-£5,000. Financial margins were tight for amateur boxing clubs at the best of times, so help was desperately needed. Public health measures undoubtedly saved millions of lives but long-term disruption to sport and social activities threatened public health in other ways, affecting mental health and physical fitness.

Many full time, part-time and spare-time professional boxers lost the reliable financial support from their sponsors in this period. The knock-on effect impeded trainers, gyms, managers and promoters. London's contender Johnny Garton had agreed to a rematch with Swansea's Chris Jenkins for the British and Commonwealth welterweight titles, only to be forced into early retirement. He needed to find a regular source of income to support his young family. The BBBoC tried to mitigate the strain, and more stories like this, by temporarily suspending license fees. Professional sport can be a short career and COVID-19 accelerated that harsh fact. There were even worries that there could be a shortage of BBBoC officials. Almost all officials worked in regular day jobs and those responsibilities conflicted with the isolation protocols required to work at post-lockdown events.

Top Rank were the first promoters to stage boxing shows behind closed doors in America. They returned as early as 9 June with mixed success. Uneven matches served the purpose of keeping their top boxers active, like WBO world featherweight champion Shakur Stevenson. They were, however, rewarded with lower than expected television ratings on ESPN, whose commentary team all worked remotely. It highlighted the issue that making competitive fights at the top level would be very difficult due to the new economic constraints, mainly linked to the loss of revenue from ticket sales. Some positives could be found and, most importantly, the first hurdles were overcome. Lessons were learned that benefitted boxing.

A 'bubble' had been set up at the MGM Grand Conference Centre in Las Vegas. Nobody could go into it without testing negative for COVID-19 and once inside it, nobody could leave until the show was over. The protocols were strict but Bob Arum, President of Top Rank, believed in them. Even at 88-years-old, Arum subjected himself to the experience to demonstrate its safety. In a show of cooperation, Arum offered the protocols and risk assessments to other promoters around the world. That selflessness wasn't routine in the business of boxing. There were positive tests over the course of Top Rank's first set of shows, most notably from WBO world super-featherweight champion Jermel Herring and 2016 Olympian Mikaela Mayer. They were both pulled out of their fights and lower-level replacements received a chance in the spotlight.

The BBBoC limited shows to just five fights in their protocols to get boxing up and running again in the UK. International travel restrictions further limited the options available for matchmakers, who were instead tasked with making more competitive domestic fights. Record building against unambitious foreign boxers was out of the window for the time being. It had been an all too common occurrence that bordered on an unnecessary rite of passage for most prospects across the country. The unintended consequence was that opportunities would be few and far between for durable domestic journeymen. Amidst the changes, United Kingdom Anti-Doping [UKAD] thought it was a good idea to publicly announce a temporary suspension of their testing programme, too. The timing and reasoning of their announcement was questionable at best.

The protocols implemented by the BBBoC meant everyone close to the action would wear some form of personal protective equipment [PPE]. Those in a boxer's corner would wear face shield visors and gloves, whilst the referee wore a mask. Sterilised spit basins were attached to disposable hose pipes and boxers also had to dispose of their hand wraps and gloves after fights. The ring was cleaned and decontaminated between fights and so were the referees, who were obligated to take quick showers before officiating another fight. A 'bubble' was required and the in-out precautions were similar to Top Rank's setup. People who travelled on public transport would be denied access and everyone had to be transferred from the hotel to the venue via designated drivers. To cement the seriousness of the new look system, a boxer's corner could only consist of the trainer and cutsman – and they all had to depart the venue immediately after the fight ended. The precautions were strict but important because no testing had 100% diagnostic accuracy and there was always the potential of false results. That was the argument used by Herring and Mayer, with some merit as Herring produced two positive results a few weeks apart. The precautions could also be undone if the people involved weren't honest or sticking to the rules – that was a critical, and the most uncontrollable, point of failure for organisers.

At first, Eddie Hearn's Matchroom, Frank Warren's Queensberry Promotions, Hennessy Sports and MTK Global were the only outfits with the financial backing to afford to operate in the UK under the new conditions. Warren was the first to return and he ended British boxing's 118-day hiatus at the BT Sport studios in London, which was devised into a one-way system marked out by red lines taped to the floor. Only 65 people could be on site and that didn't include the promoter because the 68-year-old wasn't deemed essential enough to be permitted access. It was headlined by British and Commonwealth super-bantamweight champion Brad Foster, who retained his titles after 12 rounds with James Beech Jr. There were no fans, so the boxers and judges could hear everything the corners and commentators said in a muted atmosphere. Everyone who attended was first put into quarantine at a hotel for a week and took tests, which were either swabbed from the throat or nose, or both orifices. Prenetics, a genetics testing company, carried out 104 tests for Queensberry's show and all, thankfully, were negative. That level of testing was believed to cost in the region of £20,000 – a sobering insight to the reality facing British boxing's future. Warren said it was his toughest challenge ever and that was a bold declaration given that he was shot in the chest in 1989.

Hearn announced his plans to host four shows in four weeks in August, a schedule the quick-witted promoter called 'Fight Camp.' It was no gimmick, he promised. The first rule was 'no easy fights' and it was being held in the back garden of the Matchroom mansion, the former Hearn family home that was now used as headquarter offices. It was an ominous location for away opponents, such as Trelewis' Gavin Gwynne and Cardiff's Nathan Thorley, especially when the Welshmen were originally supposed to have home advantage against James Tennyson and Chris Billam-Smith, respectively.

MTK Global booked a series of Wednesday night shows in August and September. They would take place at the Park Production Studios in South Kirby, Yorkshire – Europe's largest rehearsal space. Welsh super-lightweight champion Kieran Gething was matched with Irish lightweight champion Gary Cully and Cardiff's welterweight Maredudd Thomas would finally meet Bolton's unbeaten Sahir Iqbal for the WBC Youth title. Again, the location wasn't ideal but any boxer involved was grateful for the activity in the current climate.

It wasn't clear when crowds could return. Mass gatherings for sport were at the mercy of COVID-19 infection rates and the plans of the UK and Welsh Governments. For now, the job of the BBBoC and major promoters was just to keep boxing alive and relevant. For a long time, boxing had been a niche sport that crossed over into mainstream consciousness a couple of times a year. The task was to keep it, as safely as possible, from becoming a complete outsider.

TURF WAR! TENNYSON TAKES OUT GWYNNE IN GARDEN SHOWDOWN
Saturday 1 August 2020

Trelewis' Gavin Gwynne (12-2, 2KO) saw his second challenge for the British title end in heartbreak and backfire at the explosive hands of Belfast's James Tennyson (27-3, 23KO).

Tennyson had been stopped on three occasions at featherweight and super-featherweight, most recently in an IBF world title challenge against Tevin Farmer. Gwynne believed his size, as an established lightweight, would play a part in the fight and his gritty performance led to a thumping six-round clash on Matchroom's first show since boxing returned from the COVID-19 pandemic.

Gwynne and Tennyson shared some similarities. They were both hard working family men who started on their respective local small hall scenes. However, there was one gaping gap between them and that was how hard they hit. Whilst Eddie Hearn's pre-fight claim that Tennyson was 'the most exciting pound-for-pound puncher in world boxing" was an example of blatant promotional hyperbole, it was the Northern Irishman's immense power that made the difference.

"I had to be on my game because, at any given time, he could've landed and knocked me clean spark out," said Gwynne in acknowledgment of his uncomfortable assignment. "He was the hardest hitting person I've ever been in with and I've been in with super-middleweights. I can honestly say, he hits like a super-middleweight, that kind of power.

"He hit me with a jab early and I thought it was a backhand. I was so surprised at the amount of power he was generating. I was catching shots on my gloves and, honest to God, I'd never felt anything like it.

"As the fight was getting on, I was getting quite comfortable and I switched off for a couple of seconds. I got hit with a right hand, a hook to the side of the head, and everything went grey. I couldn't see at all and that's when I took a knee.

"I could hear the referee go 'five, six...' and I had to get up. It was still all blurry and all I remember is the ref saying 'what's your name?' and I was thinking 'what's your name?' I didn't know where I was. He's a fierce finisher and he got the job done."

The show was the first instalment of Hearn's inventive 'Fight Camp' series based in the garden of Matchroom's headquarters, a multimillion-pound mansion in Brentwood, Essex. The expensive experiment spanned four weeks and was reported to cost £5m. A canopy was erected, the type seen at stadium fights, and it was accompanied by fireworks and pyrotechnics. The extra trimmings transformed the scene into a striking outdoor venue and it resembled a luxury garden party, especially with the London skyline in the background.

There was such interest in the unique concept that plans were underway for it to become an annual occasion. The lawn might've needed relaying but Hearn, ever the opportunist, was happy the ambitious operational venture paid off, especially when talk of a television documentary series surfaced. 90 people spent the week in the 'bubble' at a nearby hotel and they were joined by a further 90 people, mainly broadcast and operations staff, on fight night. It was a boring but safe arrangement, plus it saved the boxers the effort of running around to sell tickets as usually happens in the chaotic final days before a normal show. Barry Hearn, head of the family, was banished from the garden because of recent heart operations. Instead, he was said to be watching through an upstairs window of the mansion that was once his family home.

As one of the first boxers to get the Fight Camp treatment, Gwynne was full of praise for the landmark setup. He said: "It's one to tell the grandkids. I don't think it's ever going to happen again. Being on the first show as well was a surreal experience, all of it.

"It was unbelievable, something you've never seen before. It was like walking out on a movie set, that's what it was like. He [Hearn] pulled it out of the bag. He brought boxing back."

After the boxers emerged from specially constructed changing rooms, they jabbed from long range for all of 30 seconds. Then, as expected, both squeezed up their guards and got stuck into each other – it didn't take long. At six foot, Gwynne had the height and reach to avoid a tear up but not the tendency, which suited Tennyson's tactics. Their heads came close to bumping, a symptom of the eagerness to land first, and Gwynne's facial features were further reddened by Tennyson's heavier shots.

Tennyson made a strong start to the second round and his pressure pushed Gwynne on to the ropes, whose right cross response dislodged Tennyson's gumshield. Gwynne, like countryman Craig Evans in November, was busier and had no problem finding the target. He pumped short straight punches and then introduced even shorter hooks around the sides, followed by uppercuts through the middle. It irritated Tennyson who was soon warned for using his head by referee Phil Edwards.

Gwynne continued to chip away in the third and fourth rounds, even though Tennyson's pressure was relentless and he simply didn't stop coming forward. 'The Assassin' produced 18 of his stoppages within three rounds and Gwynne was happy to get through the most dangerous part of the fight. However, Gwynne's constant output came at a cost and there was visible damage to his left eye approaching the mid-rounds.

Tennyson, a former Commonwealth and European champion, didn't appear to be getting through Gwynne's defence very often but the punches made their mark whenever he did. Tennyson stayed composed amidst an intense pace and he concentrated on damaging Gwynne, rather than outfoxing him or banking rounds. For example, Tennyson barely threw a jab in the fifth round and Gwynne tried to take advantage, bloodying his nose and pushing him on to the ropes before the bell rang. Again, the offense came at a cost for the Tony Borg trained contender. It left an opening and Tennyson landed two hard uppercuts to cause another cut, this time below Gwynne's right eye.

Sky Sports' commentary team offered backhanded compliments but Gwynne could've argued that he was narrowly ahead after five rounds. Tennyson recognised that time was ticking away and he picked his shots with more precision to start the sixth round. Springing on to the front foot, Tennyson stepped in with forceful hooks and they landed when Gwynne tried to change direction. The 30-year-old still made admirable attempts to resist Tennyson's attacks, only to be moved backwards more easily than before. Gwynne's own energy levels, usually so dependable, were being put to a test he hadn't faced before and so was his reputable toughness.

The breakthrough came when Gwynne held his left hand out to fend Tennyson off and left his chin unprotected. Tennyson's fast twitch muscle memory instantly reacted and he took the opportunity to detonate a clean right cross. It took a second or two but Gwynne eventually succumbed to the shot, kneeling for a count and the temporary chance to recover. Tennyson, a natural finisher, rushed Gwynne when he rose, twice pinning him to the ropes and swinging in hurtful hooks. It forced the referee to end the fight as Gwynne was trapped on the ropes and unable to escape.

"I think I should've stayed on the inside a bit more. When I was moving away, he caught me when my hand was down, it's my fault really," said Gwynne in his post-fight breakdown of the rights and wrongs of his performance. "I think if I stayed in there [up close], he could've tired. I hit him with a body shot in the second round and he told me he felt it. It was only 20 seconds left and the bell went.

"I thought the tide was turning and I backed him up to the ropes. I think he gave me a false [sense of] security, sort of thing. That's all down to his experience. It was only my 14th fight and he's probably had more championship fights than I've had fights, y'know what I mean? I'm still learning the game."

There was no shame in the loss and Tennyson's power could problem anyone at domestic level. Gwynne only recalled being hurt once before, during a spar with Carmarthen welterweight Dale Evans, and it was difficult to prepare for it happening mid-fight when the cameras are rolling. He was unlucky in the sense that his two British title challenges, against Joe Cordina and Tennyson, came against opponents headed for world title contention. In the latest fight, Gwynne was also without the home support originally planned for 9 May.

Hearn and Gwynne shared a few conversations in the outside area afforded to everyone in the bubble and the promoter took a shine to the Welsh champion. That support could be as influential as an arena full of fans given Hearn's role as a major powerbroker. Afterwards, he was full of praise for Gwynne's heart and other opportunities could be available in the future. There were still plans to come back to Cardiff for Lee Selby's world title eliminator in October and Gwynne was well-positioned to feature on the undercard. The Commonwealth title was vacant and it suited everyone's agenda.

"We were having some chats and I think he does like me," maintained Gwynne. "He knows I'm a genuine guy, I'm a hardworking guy. All I want is that belt and to try [financially] secure my family. He likes that sort of fighter and he knows I'm not cutting no corners. I'll put the hard work in and I think he's going to give me another shot and an easier opponent.

"Being on them shows, it raises your profile massively. Two of my last [three] fights, I've been on two of the biggest Matchroom shows and I'm not even a Matchroom fighter. I bet Matchroom fighters are getting on to Eddie and asking him 'what's the craic?' He knows I'm game and I always give a good, exciting fight. It sells to the public because of my kind of style.

"I'm not about being all brash. I'm not one of them type of guys, loud mouthing and calling people out. If they offer me a fight, I'll fight anyone, anywhere."

As a self-employed tradesman, Gwynne insisted it was worth taking unpaid time off work for the shot at becoming British champion. The father-of-one used his savings to fund family commitments during his training for Tennyson and he can always say he was a part of history. Fight Camp would certainly be one of the most unique sections of his scrapbook but Gwynne was uneasy about looking back at it too fondly. He was mindful that he didn't want to be remembered for taking part, he wanted to be remembered for winning.

"A lot of people thought I was going to pull the upset off. That's why I was gutted, letting people down… but I think I done myself justice," said Gwynne as he came to terms with the conflicting feelings of pride amidst unavoidable disappointment.

"I still feel young and I still feel like I've got plenty of years left. I haven't had wars. This is probably the only time I come out of the ring bruised up.

"I give all respect to James. He's a really nice guy and I just hope he goes on and wins a world title, if I'm honest. He deserves it and I have full respect for him."

THORLEY'S UNBEATEN BUBBLE BURST IN BILLAM-SMITH SHOOTOUT
Friday 7 August 2020

It wasn't to be for Cardiff's cruiser Nathan Thorley (14-1, 6KO), who lost his unbeaten record as a professional in an abrupt challenge to Bournemouth's Chris Billam-Smith (11-1, 10KO).

There was no 'thunder' forecast at the second week of Eddie Hearn's Fight Camp, instead it reached 30°C in Brentford, Essex. Thorley's hopes to win the Commonwealth title, having won a bronze medal at Commonwealth Games as an amateur in 2014, were burst in two rounds at the Matchroom mansion bubble.

Given the 'The Gentleman' moniker by his handlers, Billam-Smith was anything but gentle once the first bell rang. The 30-year-old surged forward and landed jabs to Thorley's body. They were accompanied by clever feints and Billam-Smith soon found his rhythm. Thorley was chased to the ropes and spent much of the opener in his shell, looking to get away from the stronger Billam-Smith, who also stepped in with hard body shots.

It looked to have settled down by the close of the round. The pair were in a loose clinch when Thorley waited for referee Mark Lyson to separate them. Billam-Smith spotted the opportunity to work when Thorley wasn't and two hard left hooks landed to the Welshman's jaw. He was buzzed and buckled to one knee, taking an eight count that coincided with the bell to end the round. It had been a torrid three minutes in Thorley's first real test since leaving the 175lbs light-heavyweight division to join the 200lbs cruisers.

Gary Lockett, in charge in the corner, implored Thorley to let his hands go and offer a deterrent. For now, that would have to wait. Billam-Smith, guided by Shane McGuigan, was looking for a quick finish. He landed quality jabs through the middle of Thorley's high guard and the Welshman was stuck in his own corner. Three consecutive right hooks landed high on Thorley's temple and he was toppled for a second time.

Thorley took the time for a few deep breaths and nodded to the referee's questions. He was ready for what would be his last stand and he finally complied with his corner's instructions to let his hands go. Billam-Smith, looking to end it, moved into range and he was met by a fast four-punch combination. Then Thorley's looping right found the target and he pushed on again. He had the space to set his feet and long straights staggered the champion on to the ropes, briefly threatening a reverse of fortunes. Sky Sports commentator Adam Smith was noticeably excited at the prospect of a dramatic turnaround but it wasn't to be.

Billam-Smith backed off to entice Thorley forwards and it tempted him to trade right hands. They threw the same shot at the same time and it was Billam-Smith who scored first, heavily knocking Thorley to the floor. The third knockdown was enough for all parties and the fight was ended after five minutes and five seconds. The early finish set Billam-Smith up for a European title shot against Belfast's Tommy McCarthy, according to Hearn.

"It was different with no crowd. Happy with the win, happy with the finish," Billam-Smith told ringside interviewer Andy Scott. "I felt as though I hurt him in the first round, not visibly but I could tell when you're landing those shots, y'know. Then obviously, I dropped him at the end of the first and I knew the finish was coming. He had a fight back in there but as soon as he had success, I knew he'd get reckless, so I just walked him on to a shot."

Along with millions of others, Thorley had been furloughed from his day job due to the COVID-19 pandemic. It allowed him to have an uninterrupted 10-week training camp as a full-time boxer, a bonus he'd rarely benefitted from in his five-year professional career. However, numerous spars with Swansea's former world champion Enzo Maccarinelli, who was planning a comeback for his 50th and final fight, couldn't compensate for Thorley's jump up in class.

Aside from a second-round knockout of Pontypridd's Jermaine Asare for the Welsh title in 2017, Thorley had competed exclusively amongst journeymen. Those opponents didn't inspire the 27-year-old and, for that reason, he had no reason to regret taking the gamble of a test like Billam-Smith, even if he wasn't ready for it.

Photo: Sacha Wiener

THOMAS TAMED IN BATTLE OF UNBEATEN PROSPECTS
Wednesday 12 August 2020

Cardiff's Maredudd Thomas (11-1, 2KO) had been asking for a step up for some time but he saw the opportunity slip through his fingers as he was tamed by Bolton's slick Sahir Iqbal (8-0, 2KO).

They engaged in an edgy eight rounder for the WBC Youth title, which was usually scheduled for 10 rounds, and Iqbal stayed a step ahead to collect a unanimous decision. It was scored 77-76, 78-75 and 78-74 in favour of Iqbal and Thomas was handed the first defeat of his professional career.

Both were keen to move on from the apprenticeship phases of their careers. The 24-year-olds were praised by onlookers for their competitive encounter, especially because two unbeaten hopefuls rarely meet that early in their careers. However, Thomas was uncomfortable in receiving praise for a losing effort and he quickly quelled his creditors.

"To me, it's a loss," clarified Thomas, rejecting the notion that were positives in his performance. "I'm gutted about that. The whole experience, fighting on a show like that, I can take that away from it and it was a close fight, to be fair, but no... I'm quite judgemental on myself and my boxing, especially when I have a loss."

Thomas' stance may soften with the passing of time but it was a fair point. As a country, Wales regularly revelled in its underdog status and victories were often claimed from valiant losses. It was a common mentality that usually resonated with non-participants, rather than the participants at the centre of sporting competition.

There were just fractions separating the welterweights, which may eventually cushion the loss for Thomas, and that was evident as early as the first round. They were both tall for the weight category and they attempted to establish their respective straight arrows. Iqbal's speedy jabs stood out in the initial exchanges and Thomas came back with his own leads in the second round. The Welshman didn't hang around, immediately closing the distance and maintaining a high punch output.

"I thought he had the first round and I had the second round," judged

Thomas. "He had a quick jab and it seemed like I was chasing him around all night. I think he definitely wanted to stay away and pick me off with the jab. I had to get in there and take it to him.

"Nothing really surprised me. He had a quick jab. It didn't have any power behind it but it was quick and snappy. Other than that, it was kind of what we expected.

"It was strange to be fighting someone taller than me because I didn't expect to get anyone taller than me in the welterweight division. He kind of had an amateur style, pitter patter and move around."

The third and fourth rounds saw Iqbal use the skills he perfected as an amateur, which helped him to secure multiple national titles as a schoolboy and youth. Thomas tried to jab to the body in an attempt to slow Iqbal's movement. Instead, Iqbal's feints offset Thomas' pressure and his crafty counters on the turn banked the sessions.

The first major breakthrough came in the fifth round. Thomas' gymmates testified that he hit far harder than his knockout ratio suggested and his right cross demonstrated the case. It froze Iqbal on impact and he was soon bundled into the ropes. A few more power punches got through before Iqbal was able to grasp tightly onto Thomas' torso. The pressure was maintained for the rest of the session and it was bumpy for Iqbal. Suddenly, they appeared near equal on the scorecards.

It was the trigger for a turning point in the fight. Iqbal's natural instinct was defensive but that tendency accelerated after he'd been buzzed. His response to Thomas' punishment wasn't to make his own mark, it was to make sure Thomas wasn't given another opening to land flush. It resulted in an astonishing 30 clinches in the rest of the fight, all of which went completely unaddressed by referee John Latham.

Iqbal, although offering a meagre offensive output, appeared to have recovered in the sixth round. Thomas continued to pursue the rangy target, only to be clipped by left hooks in between blatant and repeated clinches. The action followed a similar pattern in the seventh round. Thomas was either smothered whenever the distance shortened or picked off when he eagerly overreached.

"Everyone time I got close, he held on," said Thomas, who charged forward in the last round and finally kept a tiring Iqbal on the ropes. "I thought I could've had him out of there in the fifth [round] if he didn't hold on to me. A couple more clean shots… I could see he was hurt. He held on and done what he had to do. I think it spoilt the fight a bit.

"It was a good fight but I don't think he wanted to engage in a fight, he wanted to keep distance. When I was getting on the inside, he wanted to hold on. It is what it is really, isn't it.

"I was just chasing him. I'd have loved him to stand in the middle of the ring, box each other but after that fifth round, I don't think he wanted to get caught again. I think he was tiring as well. If it was a 10 round fight, like it should've been, it would've suited me a lot better and played into my hands."

Overall, Iqbal was effective in slowing the pace to suit his intentions. Critics will cite a reluctance to engage and his conservative approach was the antithesis to Thomas. The clever defensive methods Iqbal chose were, ultimately, approved by the referee and that was all that counted. For Thomas, he saw no reason to step back down in levels despite the result and he was keen to bounce back against the same sort of opposition.

"I don't think it was a bad loss or anything. I don't want to take a step back. If that's a 10 round fight, I honestly think I would've won it and moved on with my career.

"I don't really want to take a step back or fight journeymen. That doesn't interest me one bit. I proved I can fight at that level and he [Iqbal] was good. If I can get another fight like that, I'd love it. That's where I want to be.

"I've got to work on a few things in the gym but it's nothing major. A few little adjustments and I'll get straight back in there. When I get a date, I'll be ready. Boxing in a middle of a pandemic is something to say. It probably won't happen again… well, hopefully not anyway!"

It was MTK Global's first show since COVID-19 gatecrashed the world. The Dubai-based managerial company endured a turbulent time during the pandemic. Mainstream media openly scrutinised MTK Global's links to their co-founder, Daniel Kinahan, as his role was publicised in negotiations for Tyson Fury and Anthony Joshua's proposed unification to decide the undisputed heavyweight championship. The Irishman officially sold the company in 2017 and he then served as an independent advisor to several of their boxers. Authorities alleged that Kinahan was a senior figure in international organised crime, though he'd never been convicted of a crime.

The five-fight event took place behind-closed-doors at the Production Park Studios in South Kirkby, Yorkshire. Europe's largest rehearsal studio was an eerie setting, compounded with a row of curtained squares that served as dressing rooms. Those makeshift dressing rooms were unusually located in the same room as the ring. The strange setting was a sign of the times.

Photo: Huw Fairclough

UNDERDOG HUGHES UPSETS 'KING KONG' CARROLL
Wednesday 12 August 2020

Whilst the post-pandemic matchmaking offered by Eddie Hearn and Frank Warren was slightly more competitive than some of their usual events, it was fair to say that it hadn't actually affected the results. They promised 'no easy fights' but the sentiment of their pledge threatened to go unfulfilled. Between the pair of promoters, there hadn't been a single win from the away corner in the first five shows of British boxing's restart.

The winning streak of home corner favourites was extended for another four fights on the undercard of MTK Global's show. A non-title encounter between Ireland's uber confident Jono Carroll (18-2-1, 4KO) and Maxi Hughes (21-5-2, 4KO) headlined the show and, at the 29th time of asking, it happened – an upset, finally, from the away corner.

It took place at the Production Park Studios in South Kirby, Yorkshire. Even though Hughes resided 20 miles away in Rossington, he was very much an outsider and the oddsmakers priced him as wide as 10/1. The 30-year-old wasn't disheartened and he persuaded all three judges to side with him via 96-95, 96-95 and 97-93 scorecards. Hughes, half Welsh through his father who lived in Llanelli, landed the best win of his 10-year career after 10 calculated rounds.

"I've been about a bit. I've got experience, that's not to be frowned upon," reminded Hughes, before reflecting on his post-triumph reaction. "Some people, when they win a world or British title, say that they've climbed that mountain. I don't feel like I've climbed that mountain but it's a satisfying feeling knowing the hard work I put in has paid off.

"People say, 'Maxi is a good kid and he's always pushing the top kids' but now I've beaten a top kid, it goes to show. I've felt like I've always been able to do it, I've just not had the rub of the green. All these years of hard work have paid off now."

Carroll challenged for an IBF world title against Tevin Farmer a year ago and he pushed the American over 12 rounds. 'King Kong' then retired former world champion Scott Quigg in the weeks prior to lockdown to recement his status as a leading contender. Hughes, conversely, had been a quality domestic operator for years but he came runner up in his big fights against the likes of Liam Walsh, Sam Bowen and Martin J Ward. Few onlookers could foresee the upset when Carroll strutted to the ring and flashed a smile to the camera that was wider than the betting odds. That complacency would prove costly.

Hughes, in his own mild-mannered way, wasn't impressed with the narrative. He said: "I don't bet or do any gambling, not because I have a bad history, it's just because I'm a Yorkshireman [and] tight with money. It were only after [the fight] when some of the lads said, 'thanks for that, you've made me some good money with those odds.' Now I know them odds, I feel a bit offended.

"What makes those odds? It's bizarre! It is almost a bit offending. I'm not that interested, I don't take any notice… though if someone would've told me before, I'd have told everyone to back it.

"In the interview straight after, he was like, 'I'm not gonna take anything away from Maxi or make any excuses but… here's a big list of excuses why I lost.' I think, because I'm too humble, I stood there and listened to it. I should've said, 'hold on a minute.' I believe whatever Jono Carroll turned up with on fight night, I would've had an answer for."

The battle of southpaws began tentatively. Hughes settled quicker and he was first to land his well-schooled jab. Carroll came forward but his replies were avoided as Hughes used his savvy knowledge to slide to the sides and scoot away from danger. Sean O'Hagan, the father of IBF world featherweight champion Josh Warrington, led the corner and he was audibly pleased with the start. The role of the matador was impressively executed in the empty venue and Hughes' footwork puzzled Carroll in the early rounds.

"He says he couldn't find his rhythm or get into it but the reason is what I was doing," said Hughes, conscious that he had to take the play away from Carrol by executing a strategy based on pure boxing IQ. "It was my game plan and he wasn't able to adapt. I think that's why two southpaws didn't clash because I was able to keep him at bay.

"I'm a traditional boxer. I keep my hands tight, I work on my defence. A big part of my game is my ability to evade punches with my footwork and distance, whereas Carroll likes to be really busy and to try and let his hands go. I think he thinks he hits stronger than he does. He tries to overpower and overwhelm opponents with work rate. If my style would've been different, he might've been able to do all that."

For all of Carroll's intent in the third round, his attempts to close the distance lacked any real accuracy. Hughes' movement was coupled with sneaky backhands and it led to a crunching hook to Carroll's ribs. It was stoically sucked up and Hughes then scored with an eye-catching uppercut before the round was out to send spray from the Irishman's bold beard. Carroll was the less conventional southpaw and he was squaring up on the inside, allowing Hughes' technical ability to take advantage.

The middle rounds were closely contested. Both feinted frequently and they willed the other to take the lead. Carroll was keener and he pressed on, only to hit the gloves of Hughes' tight guard more often than he expected. There was some success in Carroll's looping left hand and Hughes had to dip very low to make them miss. Amidst Carroll's intensity and spurts of salvos, Hughes' own activity dipped and he focused on quality shots. He stepped across with a clean left cross in the sixth round and more of those sharp single punches were forecast for later on.

They both gave as good as they got in the seventh round, the difference was Hughes' insistence on having the last say before pivoting away. Carroll's straight left disturbed Hughes in the eighth round and knocked him off balance. Hughes attributed the instability to his new boots and he was quick to regain his shape. The response was an economical output and Hughes didn't want to give Carroll another chance to edge an exchange.

Hughes, with the fight still to be won, was implored to finish strong and eliminate any doubt in the last two rounds. He had regularly ventured out of his comfort zone over the last decade, demonstrated when he travelled 200 miles to be trained by Gary Lockett for a period in 2014. Now, the usually back footed boxer needed to leave his comfort zone again and do the exact opposite of his natural disposition.

Stimulated by the corner, Hughes unleashed a trio of left crosses to confront Carroll early in the 10th round and it set the tone for the final session. Those shots lacked the power to hurt Carroll but cracked hard enough to barge him backwards. The flip side of that coin was a surge of confidence through Hughes' veins as he approached the finish line.

He said: "I felt him tire, I saw him tire. Because it was so quiet, with no crowd, I could hear him breathing heavy. His corner were saying things all night to encourage him and bring him on.

"Quite early in the round, I let go an overhand backhand. It caught him and briefly hurt him. I gained some encouragement after that and I still felt fresh enough. I thought he was tired, so I'll put it on him and finish strong."

Another left cross registered in the last minute and the forthright fashion Hughes had adopted sent Carroll reeling into reverse gear. The motion was only broken when Carroll's back bounced into the ropes. It was one of the clearer rounds and, at least on two of the judges' scorecards, sealed an unexpected win.

The boxers' body language was telling when they embraced. Carroll, possibly underwhelmed by boxing behind closed doors and without fans, again wore his mandated wide smile but it was more transparent and he appeared nervous under the surface. He wasn't alone. Hughes awaited confirmation of his win and it was an unfamiliar scenario for the contender, who had come close so many times before.

"I felt it was maybe close but deep down, I knew I'd done enough to win," reassured Hughes, before he confessed last second insecurities. "I really felt I'd won but then I started getting an anxious feeling.

"It was taking a while for the judges and MC to announce the decision. I looked out of the ring and I saw the three judges together, gathering their scorecards ready to give them to the MC. I thought they were gonna do me again, it's not gonna go my way for whatever reason.

"I'd have been devastated if that [happened] because I really did think I'd won. I listened to everything Sean, my trainer, had said and everything he said Jono Carroll were gonna do, he did do it. Then I felt like it was scripted, it was my night."

Carroll would've preferred to compete at super-featherweight in more settled times. However, the match was made at lightweight and Carroll came in his heaviest for four years at 137lbs, two pounds more than Hughes. The excess weight might've explained the dip in Carroll's energy levels, which ordinarily replicated the Duracell bunny. The other explanation was that Hughes, now 30-years-old, caused the power-outage with carefully placed counters and his more refined technique.

The fight was televised across the world on iFL TV and ESPN+. Hughes, a father of one, had long paid his dues at domestic level. Now he wanted the win over Carroll to catapult him towards a shot at a significant title, even if he offered nothing but risk to future opponents. A British title loss to Sam Bowen in 2018 resulted in a low profile and short-lived retirement, which was ended when close friend Josh Warrington dethroned Lee Selby to become world champion. That spark of inspiration was repeated in the final round against Carroll as Hughes remembered the words Warrington spoke in their most recent conversation.

"I had a few months off and the birth of my daughter," said Hughes, before expanding on the turnaround in fistic fortunes. "Boxing is a short career and I still felt good enough to box at domestic level and win a title. I didn't want to get to my mid-thirties and wish I'd done it.

"Something that was going through my mind was from talking to Josh [Warrington]. He'd been giving me some advice. Last time we talked, he wished me luck and said, 'Do what you've been doing in gym and leave it all in the ring.'

"That was going through my head. What he [Carroll] was throwing back, I had my defences up and there was nowt in the punches. I thought 'I can go for this.' It paid off."

WEETCH ON THE WRONG END OF EARLY KNOCKOUT
Wednesday 26 August 2020

Cwmcarn's Jamie Weetch (12-4, 5KO) was eager to end 20 months of inactivity but his return was over far sooner than he expected.

The Welshman was last seen in a rousing points loss against Ireland's Dennis Hogan in December 2018. The Celts, both relocated to Australia, went the full 12 rounds and it prepared Hogan to challenge Jaime Munguia for the WBO world title.

A comeback fight with Queenslander Issac Hardman (7-0, 6KO) was originally agreed for six rounds and then extended to eight rounds when it was moved up the running order. The contest was given the priority status of chief support to an Australian mega-fight. Super-welterweights Tim Tszyu, son of the legendary Kostya Tszyu, and former world champion Jeff Horn squared off in the main event.

More than 16,000 people attended Queensland Country Bank Stadium in Townsville and none of them were required to socially distance or wear masks. A live audience was permitted because of the region's low COVID-19 transmission rate, making it one of the world's first major boxing events held since the start of the pandemic.

As it happened, less than one round was needed because Hardman, by name and nature, lived up to his 'headsplitter' moniker. Both were decked out in black boots, shorts and gloves, with the Australian native using the latter to dim Weetch's lights inside 90 seconds.

Perth-based Weetch usually appeared undersized for super-welterweight, so it was a surprise to see him competing as heavy as middleweight. The promoters announced the fight with just a month to go and that short notice might explain Weetch's decision to operate at 160lbs.

The size difference exacerbated Hardman's advantages. It was used to tempt Weetch into lunging forward and on to a numbing overhand right. The punch, laced with enough tranquiliser to send most middleweights to sleep, was both impressive and repulsive, depending on an individual's perception. It exploded square on Weetch's cheekbone and he fell flat on his face.

The 31-year-old seemed finished after face planting the floor. Weetch, bewildered by what hit him, groggily returned to his feet as soon as the referee's count reached two. It was possible that Weetch was acting on autopilot when he held on to the top rope to steady himself. The instinctive courage extended the fight for another 50 seconds.

The duo traded trash talk during the build-up and Weetch warned that he didn't know how to go backwards. Hardman waded in and showed him how to reverse, bullying him to the ropes to land more heavy artillery. Weetch was wobbled and downed again, this time on his knees. It obligated referee Chris Condon to intervene just as the corner threw in the towel.

At 24, Hardman's stock was rising fast. He talked well and his colourful personality promised to open doors in the future. The Brisbane-based brawler was also an undefeated mixed martial artist before he embarked on professional boxing. Hardman amassed nine wins with seven knockouts in the MMA octagon and his highlight reel featured knockouts with even more sedatives than the finish he inflicted on Weetch.

It was the first stoppage defeat of Weetch's seven-year career but not the first time he'd been down in life. When living in Wales, he was shot and stabbed in a feud with a local family. Weetch's recovery took him to a world ranking, proving he can overcome adversity and now he would have to do it again.

WOODRUFF COMES CLOSE AGAINST CLEVER CULLY
Wednesday 26 August 2020

Newport's Craig Woodruff (10-6, 4KO) launched a rocket right hand that nearly demolished Gary Cully (11-0, 5KO) but the Irish champion managed to pick himself up from the debris and navigate his way to a decision win.

Referee Phil Edwards scored the eight rounder to Cully, courtesy of a 77-75 tally, to kick off the televised segment of MTK Global's second show at the Park Production Studios in South Kirby, Yorkshire.

Woodruff was supposed to be the first Welsh boxer in action after the easing of COVID-19 restrictions. He accepted an offer to travel to Belarus and face world title challenger Isa Chaniev as part of Siesta Boxing's 'Kold Wars' series in July. However, the opportunity was lost when the BBBoC wouldn't allow Woodruff to leave the country and risk spreading COVID-19 on his return. Richie Garner, Woodruff's manager, queried the decision and later felt 'marginalised' when the BBBoC still wouldn't allow the trip but decided to accept applications from foreign boxers to appear on UK-based shows.

Pontypool's Kieran Gething was originally booked to fight Cully. A recurring elbow injury plagued Gething for a number of years and it continued to deteriorate during training. An MRI scan showed floating material in the joint and it required surgery. The Welsh champion, also born with club foot (talipes), was ruled out for the rest of 2020. That opened the door for Woodruff, an ironic circumstance given that the benefactor lost a disputed decision to Gething a year ago.

Taking on Cully, a stylish southpaw who stood well over six foot, was not an enviable task. Garner conceded that the challenge was 'a bit of a nightmare' and that was because the 24-year-old always made full use of his long physical frame. Cully kept opponents at the end of his extended reach and he established that barrier early. It was messy when they threw at the same time, mainly because of those lengthy leavers but Woodruff managed to land straight rights to the stomach. Cully responded with his trademark check hook, a hallmark of the Irish amateur team, and it was thrown as he turned away from Woodruff's work.

The pattern was set and Cully improved his lead in the following rounds. Awkward southpaw spurts were hard to avoid and they got through more often than Woodruff expected. Containing Cully's stream of constant feints became difficult and Woodruff's frustration was visible. Woodruff, in between the insights to his plateauing patience, was able to escape the single shots but Cully's more sustained combinations earned him the first half of the fight.

"Anyone who fights Cully is going to struggle," said Garner, who witnessed the skills from the comfort of the away corner. "Cully's footwork is absolutely outstanding, particularly for a southpaw. Southpaws can often appear messy and a little bit unorthodox. I didn't feel Cully fought that way at all, his footwork was outstanding. Some of the best [footwork] I've seen for a long time."

Woodruff wasn't far behind in any of the action, he just needed to shorten the gap. Cully always recognised the need to instantly reply and he did it regularly enough to cancel out Woodruff's work. It was easier to spot Cully's quality because Woodruff would retort by dropping hands and angrily calling for Cully to join him in reckless exchanges. Cully, like any smart boxer, resisted the temptation and instead took the chances to cement his lead.

"Ultimately, I'm responsible for a fighter's long-term health," reasoned Garner, well aware of his duty of care. "I certainly don't like to see fighters taking shots unnecessarily and I think he did take a lot of shots that night because he became frustrated.

"He [Woodruff] was trying to walk Cully down with his hands down to show how tough he was… I'm not really interested in how tough fighters are. I'm interested in them having a good career, preferably winning titles, making a few quid and retiring healthy. If you continue to fight like that, it's not going to happen but the positives that I can take out are the fact that he never gave up."

Garner was just as direct in his instructions to Woodruff on the night and he called for more urgency at the halfway point. Cully had measured the range and stayed away from danger up to the fifth round but he slipped up by overcommitting to a long left hand. It was easily parried by Woodruff, so the Welshman quickly reacted with his own backhand. A chopping right cross smashed into Cully's temple and it sent the unbeaten contender crashing backwards, briefly horizontal like a log hacked by a lumberjack. Woodruff, kitted out in the black and amber of his native city, suddenly threatened to cause a completely unexpected turnaround.

"I was just trying to motivate him [Woodruff] to throw more punches," revealed Garner. "The one thing he really needed to do to win that fight, when it became obvious Cully wanted to keep it long, was to punch with Cully. Throw with him and throw some more when he's in the pocket. I couldn't get Craig to do that [enough] but when he did, he had success.

"On the night, I was a bit disappointed with his discipline because he did allow himself to be frustrated but I wasn't disappointed with his power. He proved that in the fifth [round] when he decked Cully with an outrageously powerful overhand right. I think that most fighters in the division would've struggled to get up from that.

"I think, and you see this quite often in boxing, what woke him [Cully] up was the impact of hitting the floor."

Over two minutes remained in the round and Cully used an assortment of grappling techniques to kill the clock. At first, he bought time by crudely bear hugging Woodruff from behind. Then the referee was needed again because the next attack was thwarted by an uncoordinated headlock. Woodruff's swings became wild as he wrestled with Cully, who completed his recovery a minute after hitting the deck, and the moment of opportunity had passed. It was confirmed when Cully finished the round by unleashing his own accurate volleys.

Garner, no stranger to BBBoC disciplinary hearings, risked another appearance with his complaints from the corner. "I was highly critical of the referee. Even before the knockdown, the referee was letting Cully get away with holding. Craig was the stronger guy inside. Cully tried to keep things long and at a distance and then as soon as Craig came near him, he was grabbing and clutching.

"When Craig dropped him in the fifth, the holding was just absolutely outrageous. He literally clung to Craig until the end of the round and there wasn't a single warning, much to my disappointment and I let the referee know it in between rounds.

"I was screaming at the referee, to the point where I had a couple of warnings from the supervisor."

Woodruff's intent remained but the poise was removed from his punches. Instead, he swung so hard that he spun 360 degrees and gave Cully the space to skip away. Whenever Woodruff found the target, it was more of a cameo than sustained success and Cully's consistency stayed as the main difference. The eighth round followed a similar pattern and the eventually wide score didn't reflect the competitiveness of the fight.

Ever since Woodruff turned professional in 2012, the former Welsh lightweight champion had been on the outside looking in. The difference in 2020 was that he was no longer ill-prepared or being thrown to the wolves, facing the likes of Olympic gold medallist Luke Campbell on short notice as he had in 2014. In this phase of the 27-year-old's career, he was equipped with a strong support network in both his training and management. It was true that defeat to Cully, the sixth of Woodruff's career, definitely hadn't advanced his standing but, in reality, at least it didn't set him too far back either.

FINAL THOUGHTS
Tuesday 1 September 2020

When this book began, my original idea was for it to finish with the Welsh Ex-Boxers' Association [WEBA]. They provide camaraderie and a community for punchers from the past, whose stories are brought back to life and echo for current boxers and fans to learn from. In normal times, more than 200 people meet in Taff's Well on the first weekend of September for the Annual Reunion and 2020 was due to be unique. Instead of the usual event, Wales was chosen to host the British Ex-Boxers' Hall of Fame ceremony in September. The plans for a dinner event in central Cardiff were kayoed by COVID-19 and the occasion was postponed to 2021. It would be more important than ever to support WEBA whenever infection rates receded – and stabilized – to the point that public gatherings became safe again. Cyril Thomas, WEBA secretary, warned about a stagnating membership before the pandemic and COVID-19 further threatened the association's future.

The 2020 Olympics would've been a perfect fit for the finale, too. The story of Lauren Price, the world champion and jewel of Welsh amateur boxing's crown, could well have been capped with an Olympic medal. Rosie Eccles and Sammy Lee also held hopes of appearances at the Tokyo Games, now delayed to 2021. 61 boxers still awaited qualification and the patience of all would be tested until the process restarted but at least it would live another day. COVID-19 presented a more terminal threat for some amateur gyms at grassroots levels and one of this book's limitations is the absence of April's national championships. It was predictably cancelled by the national governing body, Welsh Boxing. Stakeholders could only hope that the tournament wouldn't be thinned too severely whenever amateur boxers could compete for their country's cherished red vests again in 2021.

As the 2019-2020 season wrapped up, the UK Government began test events with small numbered crowds at sporting fixtures. None of these test events involved the Welsh Government and boxing was also omitted – both would have to learn from them as a third party. The hangover from COVID-19, likely to return again in the winter, was jarringly uncertain. There was little sign that fans could attend as usual anytime soon. Except for the superstars, professional boxing in Wales did well to break even at the best of times. Now it had to somehow find a way to ensure it didn't break down altogether. This conundrum was highlighted by the six fights Welsh boxers were involved in since boxing's return from the first wave of COVID-19. All six boxers were without promoters, in the away corner and underdogs. Five of these fights ended in defeat and although that doesn't spell disaster in isolation, it wasn't a sustainable situation for the long-term health of Welsh boxing. The line 'stay ready so you don't have to get ready' was a nice soundbite and very easy to say. It was, however, an impossible task for most Welsh boxers who, in the real world, were without significant financial backing or sponsors and had real-life responsibilities just like anyone else. The reality facing most Welsh boxers was bleak and absent of the positivity this book started with.

The pandemic's pause affected Welsh boxers in a range of ways. Most notably, Liam Williams should've fought world champion Demetrius Andrade in the summer. Whilst waiting for the WBO to order purse bids for the mandatory challenge, the middleweight signed a new deal with promoter Frank Warren and agreed to stay busy. He booked himself in for a relatively safe defence of his British middleweight title against Andrew Robinson (22-4-1, 7KO) in October. Lee Selby's final eliminator for the IBF world lightweight title was, as feared, eventually impacted. Promoter Eddie Hearn proposed a 33% pay cut to opponent George Kambosos Jr and they had to take part in a purse bid when the Australian unsurprisingly opposed the new deal. Hearn won the purse bid, as it happened, but it backfired and he had to shelve out another $10,000 to secure home advantage for Selby's important autumn fight.

The pandemic was a tough time for some of the other big names of Welsh boxing. Joe Cordina took the opportunity to get surgery for a longstanding hand injury and the lightweight looked likely to suffer a year of inactivity by the time he could come back. Jay Harris was unable to build on the momentum he amassed in his WBC title challenge, whilst flyweight rival Andrew Selby announced and unannounced a short-lived retirement. The small hall scene ground to an immediate halt, unable to overcome the increased costs of staging a show that met the practicalities and protocols in place for COVID-19. Sanigar Events were rumoured to be considering a show at the S4C studios in Cardiff but the rumours were squashed as soon as they circulated.

There were some in the sport who were planning for the post-pandemic future of Welsh boxing, whenever that would be. Cruiserweight Enzo Maccarinelli promised to end four years of inactivity when it all passed. Swansea's only world champion wanted his 50th professional fight to match his 50 amateur fights, which could coincide with the opening of a new 5,000 capacity arena in the city. A featherweight title fight between Cardiff's Jacob Robinson and Carmarthen's Angelo Dragone was agreed in principle, as well as a fight between Newport's Craig Woodruff and Rhoose's Lance Cooksey. MTK Global, who were placed to promote the double header, had informed all parties that it could only happen when crowds were permitted. It was an understandable financial standpoint and reinforced that most Welsh boxers would sit on the sidelines, unless they took opportunities in the away corner on shows hosted by the UK's main promoters. Therein lay the issue, Welsh boxing was at the mercy of businessmen who had their own, more pressing priorities.

At the start of August, hopes were harboured that the cold war between Matchroom's Eddie Hearn and Queensberry's Frank Warren was beginning to thaw. Warren penned an open letter to Hearn to suggest their best boxers meet in a revolutionary act of cooperation. What the sceptics didn't forget was that, only weeks earlier, the two parties couldn't come close to an agreement for Connor Benn, son of the legendary Nigel Benn, to challenge Swansea's welterweight champion Chris Jenkins. The promoters, by the end of the month, returned to their default positions and utilised willing media platforms to challenge each other. Thankfully, the BBBoC ordered purse bids for the mandated British and Commonwealth title fight to take place by February 2021 but the rest of Warren's co-promotional ideas looked to go unfulfilled.

The business of boxing was in a prolonged period of transition. Hearn made most of the Fight Camp series free to view on Sky Sports Mix, which was available without a paid-for subscription. Boxing's return was met with lower-than-expected television audiences on both sides of the Atlantic. Hearn's efforts to boost viewing figures wasn't an anomaly, everyone had to go the extra mile to maintain interest in the sport. Boxing was, for once, forced to think beyond the short-term. The paying public had competing priorities and it was no surprise that boxing suffered during an economic downturn. Hearn could talk his way out of a straitjacket, but those verbal Houdini skills were up against boxing's legacy of unsustainable models that built little loyalty with its casual fanbase. The uncomfortable truth was that hardcore fans, who will always support boxing, didn't exist en masse. That was why the secondary businesses that rely on boxing were also in danger. In a depressing sign of the times, the highly regarded Boxing Monthly magazine ceased publication during the pandemic after 30 years of life, such was the strain on the economy.

As disappointing as the end of the 2019-2020 season was for Welsh boxing, it's important to provide perspective. Boxing was, by a long shot, not the main victim of the pandemic. 41,614 deaths and 362,000 cases had been recorded in the UK by 1 September. Millions were affected worldwide and the end still wasn't in sight. It was, if anything, only due to get worse in the winter.

Obviously, it goes without saying that I didn't expect the inaugural Welsh Boxing Annual to include a worldwide pandemic. Covering the knock-on effects COVID-19 had on Welsh boxing was, nonetheless, an important chapter of our history. I also didn't expect this book to chronicle a failed doping test, an alleged fixed fight, bereavement or the subject of mental health – all of which received careful consideration. Amidst all of that turmoil, it's worth remembering that there were plenty of reasons for positivity in the first half of the 2019-2020 season, such as the crowning of Wales' 13th world champion.

I'm extremely thankful to all of those who made themselves available for interview and shared their stories, as well as the inspirations and sacrifices that underpinned their successes. Many were spoken to in the immediate aftermath of their fights and I'm especially grateful to those who made themselves available when they were enjoying well-deserved time with family. As I mentioned in the opening acknowledgements, boxers make for the most authentic of subjects and this book benefitted from that transparency. That's not to say boxing doesn't have its own repetitive clichés. "Styles make fights" and "sparring is sparring" remain popular soundbites but they're forgivable because they're often true.

My final thanks go to you, whoever you are, for picking up this book. Fans are the cornerstone of any sport and this is especially the case in boxing. Your interest in this book and Welsh boxing is enormously valued.

- Dewi Powell

Printed in Great Britain
by Amazon